Praise for *Pigeons:*

"Blechman is a talented observer and a light-on-his feet writer. He deftly carves the interesting from the extraneous . . . this is as intimate a profile of pigeons as you'll ever read."
—*The San Diego Union-Tribune*

"Blechman is adroit in his attention to minutiae, and breezy with his prose, and he sets the right tone early: he's both journalistic and amused." —*Time Out Chicago*

"A quick and thoroughly entertaining read, *Pigeons* will have readers chuckling at the quirky characters and pondering surprising pigeon facts." —*Audubon Magazine*, Editor's Choice

"Consistently engaging and surprising . . . *Pigeons* manages to illuminate not merely the ostensible subject of the book, but also something of the endearing, repellent, heroic, and dastardly nature of that most bizarre of breeds, Homo sapiens." —Salon.com

"If ever there was a creature that was due a revisionist assessment, it is the pigeon. Andrew Blechman's wonderful book gives the lowly bird its due, but along the way reveals as much about humans—with our bizarre, sometimes obsessive love-hate relationship to this most enduring of birds—as the pigeons themselves. In so doing, he has written one of those rare and magical books that cause the reader to see the world differently. Read *Pigeons* and you'll never look at Trafalgar Square, the Piazza San Marco, or Bryant Park the same way again."
—Warren St. John, author of *Rammer Jammer Yellow Hammer: A Road Trip Into the Heart of Fan Mania*

"Enjoyable and informative book . . . while Blechman's book won't convert pigeon haters to pigeon lovers, it does make for entertaining reading." —*Publishers Weekly*

"An enjoyable read." —*Library Journal*

"Few of us who live in cities, besieged by flights of what we like to call winged rats, can rightly be described as philoperisterons. But King George the Fifth of England was. So was Charles Darwin. Julius Reuter was too, though for purely commercial reasons. And so also, and for which we should all be thankful, is Andrew Blechman. Mr. Blechman positively loves pigeons—but as graceful and ancient grey doves, not as either targets or as food. In this breezy, quirky, endlessly entertaining book, he tells us just why—and explains why philoperisteronicism is, generally speaking, a Good Thing."

—Simon Winchester, author of *The Professor and the Madman*

"No doubt the birds evoke a wide range of emotions among people. And whichever side a person might fall on, Blechman's well-reported findings will leave him better informed about pigeons and the multi-layered culture that results." —Associated Press

"I've been as guilty as anybody of looking down on the lowly Rock Dove. But Andrew Blechman's *Pigeons* woke me up. Informative and well-written, if anybody can read his book and still harbor contempt for pigeons, I have to wonder if there is hope for human beings."

—Mark Bittner, author of *The Wild Parrots of Telegraph Hill*

"Andrew Blechman's writing is graceful and swift like his subject. The ubiquitous pigeon, whose image spans the lows and highs of human imagination, finds a superb chronicler, exegete, partisan, and redeemer in this book....This book proves, once again, that magic is near at hand, that it can feed from our hands, and that there are mottled angels in our midst. Read *Pigeons*—it's marvelous."

—Andrei Codrescu, author of *New Orleans, Mon Amour* and commentator for NPR's *All Things Considered*

"You can love them or hate them, and even shoot, feed, race, or eat them, but if you ever ignore pigeons as a major natural force, you will surely be splattered upon. After trailing these remarkable creatures from the rooftops of Queens to the castle of a queen, Andrew Blechman has bagged a story that is fun, warm, and full of wonder."

—Mark Obmascik, author of *The Big Year: A Tale of Man, Nature, and Fowl Obsession*

Pigeons

PIGEONS

The Fascinating Saga of the World's Most Revered and Reviled Bird

Andrew D. Blechman

Grove Press
New York

Printed in the United States of America
Published simultaneously in Canada

Library of Congress Cataloging-in-Publication Data

Blechman, Andrew.
Pigeons / Andrew Blechman.
p. cm.
ISBN-10: 0-8021-4328-8
ISBN-13: 978-0-8021-4328-0
1. Pigeons. I. Title.
QL696.C63B58 2006
598.6'5—dc22
2006043709

Grove Press
an imprint of Grove/Atlantic, Inc.
841 Broadway
New York, NY 10003

Distributed by Publishers Group West

www.groveatlantic.com

07 08 09 10 10 9 8 7 6 5 4 3 2

For Lillie Annabelle
I love you to the moon and back again.

Contents

If you have men who will exclude any of God's creatures from the shelter of compassion and pity, you will have men who will deal likewise with their fellow men.

—St. Francis

What's this fuss I hear about an Eagle Rights Amendment . . . ? Why I think the eagle has been treated fair enough. . . . Between you and me, if we give eagles rights, the next thing you know, we'll have to give rights to pigeons. . . . Why, you won't be able to get a seat in the park. It will be the birds sitting on the benches throwing us little pieces of toast.

—Gilda Radner

Introduction: Pigeonholed

Some days you're the pigeon. Some days you're the statue.

—Anonymous

FOR MUCH OF MY LIFE, I DIDN'T HAVE A STRONG OPINION about pigeons. At best, I found their incessant bobbing and waddling mildly charming to watch as I walked through the streets of New York City. It was my college girlfriend who first alerted me to their nefarious lack of hygiene. They may *look* harmless, she informed me, but they're actually insidious carriers of hidden filth—"rats with wings"—that eat garbage off the streets and crap in their own nests.

Lamenting the city's lack of wildlife, I hung a bird feeder from the fire escape outside my barred windows in an effort to attract songbirds to my apartment. The feeder didn't attract robins or cardinals, but it was popular with pigeons. They flocked to my fire escape, landing in friendly, cooing clusters. They were animated, fun to watch, and they kept me company as I looked out onto an otherwise drab urban vista.

A few days later, I noticed my superintendent standing on the sidewalk contemplating the sudden rise in bird droppings around the building's entrance. I suspected I was in trouble when he looked up at my window and spied the bird feeder. He bounded up the fire escape, gave me a look

1

of enraged incredulity, and promptly pitched my feeder onto the sidewalk below, where it exploded into a cloud of birdseed shrapnel. My nature experiment was clearly over.

Months after, I got a taste of pigeon prejudice firsthand. I was interviewing for a job outside Rockefeller Center when I felt a splat on my head and then, seconds later, several oozy drips down my ear and onto my freshly pressed white shirt. I was at a complete loss, too embarrassed to survey the damage. Could I just pretend it had never happened?

I sat there motionless, unsure what to do, and keenly aware of everyone else around me. It was as if the whole plaza had suddenly gone silent, all eyes focused on me— the crap-covered stooge. I reached for a napkin, but we were eating falafel sandwiches, and mine was already covered in tahini. My interviewer looked at me in stunned silence, face frozen in horror, eyes fixated on the gooey mess. "Oh, my," he managed. "Oh, my."

Then I met José Martinez. It was a dreary day, the sidewalks covered in graying slush. I was waiting in line at the corner bodega to pay for a tuna sandwich when I struck up a conversation with the man next in line. I have no idea how we started talking about pigeons, but this was New York City, after all, where pigeons are not an altogether unusual topic of discussion. He told me about his brother Orlando's loft of racing pigeons.

"Racing pigeons?" I asked. Did he mean like the scruffy pigeons in the street that crap all over the city's buildings? Had I misunderstood him? People don't race birds—do they?

"My brother's pigeons are like thoroughbreds," José replied. Pigeon thoroughbreds? The following day, armed with a pen and notebook, I journeyed to Orlando's home in Brooklyn to meet the pigeon man myself.

Alternating between enthusiasm for my project and frustration with my seemingly endless stupid questions, José's brother nonetheless opened up his pigeon-centric world to me. I spent a year with Orlando, tagging along with him to the very first stirrings of a new racing season and all the way to one of the biggest races of the year. The Bronx-based Main Event is the Kentucky Derby of the New York pigeon-racing community. At stake is over $15,000 in prize money for the first-place finisher (plus tens of thousands more in side bets) and a year's worth of bragging rights for winning one of the metro area's most competitive races.

Orlando put it to me this way: "To walk into your racing club, knowing that your bird beat out a thousand others because you put in the time, bred it right, fed it right, and trained it right, well, few things compare."

But the Main Event was nearly a year off. First Orlando would spend an anxious year earnestly preparing for the big race. Orlando had won it once before, and consequently, he had a lot at stake this time around, including his cocky reputation.

These were my first steps into the pigeon universe and its shaggy patchwork of obsessive subcultures. As I've journeyed through the world of pigeons, I've found that this seemingly unremarkable bird routinely evokes remarkably strong reactions. While most animals trigger universally similar emotions—puppies are "cute and cuddly"; cockroaches are "disgusting"—the pigeon somehow spans both extremes.

No animal, I discovered, has developed as unique and continuous a relationship with humans as the common pigeon. Nor is there any animal that possesses such an unusual array of innate abilities seemingly designed for our utilization.

The fanatical hatred of pigeons is actually a relatively new phenomenon. Far from being reviled, pigeons have been revered for thousands of years. After all, whom do we celebrate as Noah's most loyal passenger if not the white dove bearing an olive branch and bringing hope? ("Pigeon" is merely a French translation of the English "dove.") Although now scorned, those so-called filthy and annoying pigeons in your local park have an unparalleled history and an unmatched intelligence.

Consider this:

They've been worshipped as fertility goddesses, representations of the Christian Holy Ghost, and symbols of peace;

They've been domesticated since the dawn of man and utilized by every major historical superpower from ancient Egypt to the United States of America;

It was a pigeon that delivered the results of the first Olympics in 776 B.C. and a pigeon that first brought news of Napoleon's defeat at Waterloo over twenty-five hundred years later;

Nearly a million pigeons served in both world wars and are credited with saving thousands of soldiers' lives;

And although it is often overlooked, it was upon the backs of pigeons that Darwin heavily relied to support his theory of evolution.

Pigeons are athletes of the highest caliber. While racehorses receive all the glory, with their 35 mph sprints around a one-mile racetrack, homing pigeons—a mere pound of flesh and feathers—routinely fly over five hundred miles in a single day at speeds exceeding 60 mph, finding their way home from a place they've never been before, and without stopping for food or water.

Pigeon racing is an internationally popular sport that counts the queen of England among its enthusiasts. Winning birds can bring home millions of dollars in prize money and fetch tens of thousands of dollars at auction.

Then there's the bird's culinary reputation as one of the world's finest meats—the milk-fed veal of the sky— treasured by chefs the world over and served nice and rare at many of the finest restaurants.

Although we all share a universal bond with this ubiquitous bird, there are some of us whose lives revolve around the pigeon in more profound—and often humorous—ways. I met trainers who ran around their backyards with whistles in tow, barking orders at their racing pigeons as if conditioning a team of professional soccer players; militant members of a New York City pigeon underground who prowl city streets in search of pigeon poachers; and backyard geneticists who toyed with the cellular composition of pigeons, in their quest to create a bird more akin to a Dresden figurine than a child of nature. I was fascinated by their obsession with what I believed to be a scruffy looking bird with a brain the size of a lima bean.

For better or worse, the lives of man and pigeon are inexorably intertwined. Like dogs and cats, they are a product of our own domestication and follow us wherever we go. From a farmer's fertile fields to an urbanite's concrete cities, the pigeon is our constant and inescapable companion. Wherever humans go, they're likely to find a flock of pigeons loafing nearby.

Frankly, I didn't know chicken scratch about pigeons when I started this book—I mistook the call of a mourning dove for an owl because it went "who, who, who." My quest for all things pigeon was surprisingly peripatetic and landed me in a variety of unusual situations. I found myself hesitantly scaling the dung-riddled walls of a medieval English dovecote; eating tacos outside a Phoenix "titty bar" in the hopes of scoring an interview with pigeon enthusiast Mike Tyson; and blasting away at live pigeons with a hefty shotgun in a Pennsylvania sportsmen's club.

And yet, until I accidentally stumbled into the passionate world of pigeons, I barely noticed them. Like many urban dwellers, I viewed pigeons as just another fact of city life—so common, so ubiquitous—that I often looked right past them.

The domestic pigeon lives both in the relative luxury of the queen of England's racing lofts and feeds off discarded pizza crusts and doughnuts on the streets of New York City. They are both descendants of *Columba livia*, the rock dove. Very loosely translated, the Latin name means a "leaden-colored bird that bobs its head." The rock dove (the name "rock pigeon" is becoming increasingly popular among ornithologists) is a member of the family *Columbidae*. Other members of this family include the mourning dove, the turtle dove, the wood pigeon, and the ill-fated passenger pigeon. If you trace your finger a little further back along this family tree, you'll see that the rock dove is even related to the extinct dodo bird.

All members of *Columbidae* share several distinct attributes. They generally have plump bodies, small (often bobbing) heads, and stubby legs, as well as short slender bills with a fleshy covering, or "cere." All of these birds make distinctive cooing sounds, live in loosely constructed nests, and lay two white eggs at a time that are incubated by both parents. Both sexes also produce a milklike substance in their throat, or "crop," which they feed to their newborns. While all other birds collect water in their beaks and tip their heads back to drink, pigeons suck their water like a horse at a trough.

Although a pigeon and a dove are the same bird, the more delicate members of the family are called doves, while the seemingly less graceful members of *Columbidae* are also called pigeons, hence the old adage that all pigeons are doves but not all doves are pigeons. "Dove" has come to mean petite and pure. Colloquial usage of the word "pigeon," on the other hand, emphasizes the bird's docile nature and places it in a negative light. "Stool pigeon" is synonymous with stooge, and to be "pigeonholed" is to be arbitrarily stereotyped in a disparaging manner. Pigeons themselves, it would seem, have been pigeonholed as dimwitted. Such is the linguistic discrimination that a large pigeon will nevertheless be called a dove simply because it is white. This lack of pigment is often confused for virtuousness—a characteristic that few are willing to link with an ordinary pigeon. Perhaps we can pin the linguistic confusion on William the Conqueror, whose Norman victory at the Battle of Hastings ensured that the English language would be peppered with French synonyms.

Despite this linguistic bias, the unassuming pigeon is truly special. It doesn't live in trees but prefers nesting on rocky ledges (although a window ledge will do just fine). And unlike its distant relations, it will never abandon its nest, developing a keen sense of homing to ensure its return. It breeds enthusiastically in captivity and is naturally gregarious, enjoying the company of its own kind, even in close quarters. In the wild, a pigeon lives only about three or four years. But in the relative safety of captivity, a pigeon can live over twenty years.

With hollow bones containing reservoirs of oxygen, a tapered fuselage, giant breast muscles that account for one third of its body mass, and an ability to function indefinitely without sleep, the rock dove is a feathered rocket built for speed and endurance. If an average up-and-down of the wing takes a bird three feet, then a racer is making roughly 900,000 of those motions during a long-distance race, while maintaining 600 heartbeats per minute—triple its resting heart rate. The rock dove can reach peak velocity in seconds and maintain it for hours on end. One pigeon was recorded flying for several hours at 110 mph—an Olympian feat by any measure. Clearly these birds aren't designed to jump around branches or glide on warm air currents; they're designed for rapid yet sustained flight. Their fuel? Richly oxygenated blood, just one ounce of birdseed a day, and a hardwired need to return home.

Athletic prowess aside, *Columba livia* is also an inexplicably obliging bird and incredibly easy to domesticate. If you hold one in your hands, it won't struggle or bite. And if you let one go, it will always return home. It is these qualities that have led to the rock dove's unique and unrivaled relationship with humans, making it the world's first domesticated bird.

Cultural reminders of this connection are abundant. The bird's holographic form graces many of our credit cards. Its outline is used to sell soap, chocolate, greeting cards, and world peace. Rock doves have graced films: Marlon Brando found solace caring for them in *On the Waterfront,* and "Mr. Smith" even brought his pigeons with him to Washington. For years, dramatically circling pigeons were a celebrated attraction at Walt Disney World. Picasso painted them frequently and named his daughter Paloma—Spanish for pigeon.

The rock dove has been our companion for thousands of years. Like most birds, the pigeon is basically a feathered reptilian dinosaur and has roamed the earth in one form or another for over 30 million years. By comparison, we've been walking about for a mere 130,000 years.

As a particularly successful species, the rock dove has come to populate every continent on earth, with the exception of Antarctica. In the early 1600s, French settlers imported the rock dove to the New World for meat. Now they populate nearly every city in the Western Hemisphere, from the arid deserts of Arizona to the frigid climes of Alaska. The pigeon does not migrate but rather adapts to its chosen location year-round.

Fossil evidence suggests that the pigeon originated in southern Asia and made its way across northern Africa and Europe, much like the Muslim conquerors and the Mongol hordes of yore. Skeletal remains found in Israel confirm the rock dove's existence there for at least three hundred thousand years.

When did human fascination with the pigeon arise? Most likely with our earliest days as cavemen. Although the rock dove generally prefers sea cliffs with protective ledges, it probably made itself at home in the outer nooks and crannies of our shallow caves and then scavenged for our crumbs. It's also quite likely that humans ate the tasty little bird whenever possible.

This somewhat symbiotic relationship progressed along with human civilization. As we learned to domesticate grains and cereals, we inadvertently domesticated the pigeon as well. As any farmer knows, a small portion of every crop never makes it to the granary. Rather, bits and pieces of it spill to the ground during harvest. These leftovers make for easy pigeon pickings. Crevices in our mud and stone farmhouses also made for good nesting places. It could be said that the pigeon domesticated itself and humans merely met it halfway, often with a healthy appetite.

Research suggests that the pigeon was domesticated perhaps as early as ten thousand years ago, not long after we tamed our other "best friend," the dog. While the bird remains somewhat cautious, it is inherently unafraid of humans. As anyone who has befriended a pigeon will tell you, it doesn't take much effort to train the bird to eat out of your hand. In fact, a pigeon will happily walk through your front door if it knows there is birdseed inside. Conversely, given that pigeons can be bred all year long and are naturally docile, they were ideally suited to become a domesticated food source.

Eventually, early humans built homes for their pigeons, called dovecotes, and harvested the bird for food on a regular basis. They were crude structures at first, but by the late Middle Ages, dovecotes were built with great architectural flourish. Thousands of these spectacular dovecotes still dot the European countryside, often attached to country manor houses and estates.

The vast majority of today's feral pigeons can be traced to the proliferation of these dovecotes across Eurasia.

Wealthy Romans were particularly fond of pigeon meat, so dovecotes were introduced throughout their empire (as were garlic, asparagus, and other delicacies). Since dovecotes are designed to allow pigeons to come and go as they please, some pigeons inevitably wandered off. Roman buildings and monuments were also populated with feral pigeons, much like the pigeons of St. Mark's Square in Venice and London's Trafalgar Square today.

Mesopotamian cuneiform tablets mention the domestication of pigeons over five thousand years ago, as do Egyptian hieroglyphics. In human terms, the pigeon's most useful skill—its innate ability to "home"—was perhaps first recognized and utilized by ancient Mediterranean seafarers. Although the bird often dwells on coastal cliffs, it has an aversion to large bodies of water and always flies inland in search of food. A bird released from a ship will quickly orient itself to land, and early sailors undoubtedly followed suit.

It was only a matter of time before humans learned to further manipulate the bird's homing skills and use them for delivering messages. Egyptians may have been the first to use pigeons as carriers when they sent birds in the four cardinal directions to announce the ascension of a new pharaoh to the throne. Likewise, messages regarding flood levels were sent up and down the Nile by means of an early pigeon post. King Solomon is said to have made use of a pigeon post for critical messaging, and archaeologists have found underground pigeon coops in Israel from this period that held an estimated 120,000 birds.

By the eighth century B.C., pigeons were used regularly by the Greeks to carry messages, particularly results of the Olympic games to the various city-states. As

11

impractical as the use of birds in relaying messages may sound, consider the alternative. According to Greek legend, it took most of a day for the news of the Persian defeat at Marathon to reach Athens—a mere 26.2 miles —and then the runner died from exhaustion.

By 500 B.C., the emperor of China was regularly receiving messages in Beijing from outer provinces. A bird could deliver a message in as many hours as it took a horse and rider days. Hannibal employed pigeons during his siege of Rome, and Julius Caesar utilized them to relay messages from his military campaigns in Gaul. Genghis Khan and his grandson Kublai Khan created a pigeon post that spanned one sixth of the world. For thousands of years, the fastest way to send a message was by pigeon. They were the avian equivalent to today's Fed Ex, and the governments and militaries of every major historical power exploited them as such.

Throughout history, the bird's unusual talents and fecundity earned it respect. But it was probably the bird's affectionate nature that earned it adoration and made it integral to religious worship since the beginnings of human civilization in Mesopotamia.

In many ways, pigeons exhibit the tender traits we most admire in ourselves. The Jewish Bible's Song of Solomon speaks of the bird lovingly, in anthropomorphic terms: "O my dove, that art in the clefts of the rock, in the secret places of the stairs, let me see thy countenance, let me hear thy voice; for sweet is thy voice, and thy countenance is comely."

When two pigeons court, they link beaks in a manner that looks a lot like kissing. The birds are actually exchanging food. The female playfully places her beak inside the male's beak to signal that she expects the male to care for her and, soon, their children. By accepting the female's beak—and this is where we humans differ—the male is accepting his impending responsibility and not just recreational nookie. When pigeons mate, they mate for life. ♡

The sexual act itself is relatively gentle and completely consensual. A duet of affectionate cooing follows, as well as a careful preening of each other's feathers. In a demonstration of true gender equality, the parents share domestic duties and spend an equal amount of time sitting on the eggs and feeding their young. A happy couple can raise as many as twelve to eighteen babies a year. This cooperative behavior and frequent mating, coupled with the bird's ability to live peacefully in large flocks, led to its reputation for fruitfulness and purity of spirit.

One of the earliest known mother-goddesses was the Sumerian, and later Babylonian, goddess Ishtar, "queen of heaven and earth and of the evening star." She is often depicted either holding a pigeon or as the winged bird herself. The Phoenician goddess of love and fertility, Astarte, was also symbolically represented as a pigeon, as were the Greek goddess Aphrodite and the Roman goddess Venus.

In the Sumerian *Epic of Gilgamesh*, which predates the Hebrew Bible by hundreds of years, there is also a great flood in which the pigeon plays the role of messenger. The rock dove's message—of subsiding waters and thus new beginnings and new hope—lent the pigeon its role as the bird of peace.

Although the pigeon was cherished for its innocent and gentle nature, these same attributes caused the bird to bear the brunt of brutal ritual sacrifice in humans' quest for spiritual atonement and divine appeasement. It is recorded that Ramses III offered 57,810 pigeons to the god Ammon at Thebes. Besides a talent for assembly-line slaughter, the offering also reveals an Egyptian knack for domestication.

The Jewish Bible describes the bird as a poor person's offering at the Jerusalem temple. If you couldn't afford a heifer, goat, or lamb, then the sacrifice of two pigeons would do just fine—one for a sin offering, the other for a burnt offering. According to the Gospels, when Mary and Joseph visited the temple after the birth of their son Jesus, they made an offering of pigeons. Thirty-three years later, pigeon sellers were among the vendors that Jesus berated when he marched through the temple.

The Hebrew God nonetheless appreciated the pigeon offerings. In fact, when sealing His covenant with Abraham and his descendants, He specifically asked Abraham to sacrifice (along with a collection of larger domesticated animals) a young pigeon, or squab, particularly prized for its tender flesh, as the baby is eaten before it ever has a chance to spread its tiny wings.

In Christian writings and art, the bird is given the pious honor of symbolically representing the Holy Spirit, in much the same way a guiltless lamb represents Jesus. When the Holy Ghost visits the Virgin Mary to impregnate her, he does so in the form of a pigeon. The bird is often depicted in Christian art as descending from heaven in a bolt of light that ends in Mary's stomach or head.

The pigeon is also present for Jesus' ritual immersion into the river Jordan by John the Baptist. Writes Luke,

"And the Holy Ghost descended in a bodily shape like a dove upon him, and a voice came from heaven, which said, Thou art my beloved Son; in thee I am well pleased." A pigeon attends Jesus' crucifixion, perhaps as a reminder that God has not abandoned his son. Muhammad is also said to have been fond of pigeons, and to this day the bird continues to hold a protected place in Islamic society. Chinese society also reveres the pigeon. One tradition, hundreds of years old, celebrates the bird in a most unusual manner: intricately carved gourds are attached to specially trained pigeons. The gourds act as whistles of varying octaves and notes, playing music as the birds circle above.

Throughout history, the bird has been treasured as a source of companionship (and protein), admired and utilized for its unique navigational and athletic abilities, and even worshipped as a timeless symbol of God's grace. We release them as offerings of hope at our weddings and civic ceremonies, and as a representation of the soul's final journey at our funerals. Yet we have brutalized them at the sacrificial altar, slaughtered more than one species to extinction, and continue to heap daily abuse onto the ones still in our midst.

As I threaded my way through the peculiar world of pigeon people, I found this ambivalence magnified. Although I still had no firm opinion on the bird's place in the avian pantheon, there were plenty of people out there who did. Their minds were made up. Some coddled and preened them; others pulverized them for sport. It was a winter that thrust me onto the front lines of extreme eccentricity and fierce brutality. Like the bird, I was caught in the middle. Passive participation and detached indifference were no longer possible. I would be sucked into the pigeon's universe in ways that I never could have suspected nor embraced.

Winter

1

Old Cocks

IT'S ANOTHER BRUTALLY COLD AND WINDY DAY, THE SKY A
lifeless dull gray. José's brother, Orlando Martinez, parks
his truck outside a small run-down cinder-block building
beneath the Brooklyn-Queens Expressway and warms his
hands on the dashboard vents. A sign reads BOROUGH PARK
HOMING PIGEON CLUB, EST. 1924.

It's the first club meeting of the new race season.
Orlando had suggested I attend this meeting, but now he's
starting to regret bringing me along. He takes a deep breath
and removes his keys from the ignition. "I have to warn
you. All we do at these meetings is fight. We should have
come wearing hard hats and bulletproof vests."

Inside there are a few battered benches, discarded
school chairs, and a Coke machine that sells Budweiser.
A collection of gold trophies capped with regal-looking
pigeon figurines sits on a shelf just beneath the water-
stained drop ceiling. A few dozen men, ranging from
their early twenties to their late seventies, mill around an
old feather-encrusted kerosene heater. One man chews
on an extinguished cigarette butt, flipping it around with
his tongue. It's a rough-looking bunch, and they eye me
suspiciously.

Orlando, with his natural buoyancy, easy charm, and boyish smile, stands out from the crowd. His boisterous enthusiasm and loud wisecracks are generally out of step with the club's pervasively dour mood. Despite being in his mid-forties, Orlando shows few signs of traditional maturing. His olive skin is smooth and nearly unwrinkled; he regularly dresses in sneakers and jeans, works erratically, and lives with his mother as well as his chatty young wife, Omayra, more than twenty years his junior.

He struts around the room as if running for political office, playfully slapping backs, throwing fake punches, and showing off his custom-embroidered jacket depicting a gray pigeon with red feet and the words "OJ Loft" (for Orlando and José's racing team, or "loft"). He gets into a discussion about pigeon feed with his friend Sal. "Don't get me wrong, it's clean feed," Orlando says. "But I still think it's garbage."

John Ferraro, the club's large and occasionally ill-tempered president, sits behind a picnic table and calls the meeting to order. He's in a particularly foul mood today, perhaps owing to the facsimile of him that Orlando is passing around: "John Ferraro, wanted for molestation of pigeons. Last seen with a red-checker hen between his legs."

The first order of business is termites. The club's basement is full of them. After some rancorous debate, the members agree to hire an exterminator. Next item is the scheduling and cost of shipping birds. Shipping dates can be a tempestuous topic, because they form the framework upon which the entire racing season is built. The birds are typically dropped off at the club on a Friday night; trucked overnight to a destination, say, three hundred miles away; then released in the morning.

When members check over the shipping schedule, they see that the Northeast Union, an organization that represents all the area race clubs, has scheduled a shipping the same night as the Viola—another popular autumn race with a guaranteed first-place prize of $30,000. That means club members are stuck preparing their birds for one race while welcoming birds home from another. The "fucks" start flying. "I'm tired of us getting fucked up the ass," says a voice in the crowd. "We've done everything but bend down for these motherfuckers," says another. Orlando winces.

To the uninitiated, it may seem like a minor problem, but shipping day is critical. Any racer worth his bag of pigeon feed will spend hours prepping his birds for the Viola, let alone the Main Event. Shipping is a full-day project for Orlando. He spends the morning monitoring the winds aloft and other weather data online so he can judge his birds' nutritional needs. "If it's a hot day, I'll feed them accordingly. For tough race days, I load them up like marathoners on fats, proteins, and carbs. I'll feed them peanuts and safflower seeds. Sometimes I'll give them B-12, amino acids, and brewers yeast. If it's a short race, I'll give them plenty of corn and peas. Picture a boxing trainer. That's what I am."

After the feeding, Orlando concentrates on heightening the birds' motivation with intimacy. Two hours before shipping, he sets out clay nesting bowls and removes a partition in his rooftop coop separating the cocks from the hens. After mere minutes of romance, the birds are again placed into separate compartments, so Orlando can capitalize on their sexual frustration.

"Coming home to food is a big motivator, but pussy's even bigger," Orlando informs me. "I've given up

21

a lot of meals for pussy." As he packs the birds one at a time into the shipping crates, keeping the cocks and hens separate, Orlando gives each bird eye- and nose drops to help clear their nasal passages.

It's obvious that few club members flying birds in the Viola are willing to ship birds that same day. So club members are stuck footing the cost of an additional shipment. "Look around," Ferraro says. "Everybody's on a fixed income. We got to keep our costs down. We're here to make money. That's what it's all about." Members ask Ferraro to look into the matter.

Ferraro wants to talk about technology next. He is trying to convince club members to buy electronic clocks. Currently, when a bird comes home from a race, its owner takes a numbered elastic band off its ankle. The band goes into a capsule and is then placed into a tamper-proof clock, where it is time-coded and stored for safekeeping. The system makes cheating all but impossible, a vital consideration given the fanaticism of racers and the high stakes of some pigeon races.

"Last year I told you electronic clocks were the system of the future," Ferraro says. "Now they're the present. The Maspeth club's using them. So are the Triboro, Long Island, and Nassau clubs. Suffolk is going to start using them next week. These new clocks are unbelievable. They work like an E-ZPass. You put a chip on the bird and the clock scans it as soon as the bird comes in. It even has a built-in master timer that automatically updates using satellites. Next thing it'll be online. No mistakes, no cheating."

The new clocks automate many of the tedious but necessary tasks performed after the races. When the pigeons come home, everyone has to bring their clocks and time-stamped racing bands to the clubhouse so they can be manually entered into the club books and then into a computer that calculates a bird's average speed. Because lofts are located at varying distances from a race's starting point, the first bird home isn't necessarily the winner. As the saying goes, it's a sport with one starting gate and thousands of finishing lines. A certified aerial survey is performed on each loft, and its distance from the race's starting point is precisely calculated to the thousandth of a mile. The winner is the bird with the fastest average speed.

It's a time-consuming process performed by a dwindling membership. Waiting for your pigeons to come home is fun. So is being declared a winner. Entering race data isn't. "Nobody wants to do the work, and there aren't a lot of us left to do it," Ferraro tells me after adjourning the meeting. "Not too many years ago, we used to fill this place up. Now there's nobody—just twelve active members. It's a dying sport."

A week later, many of the Borough Park club members gather at another racing club—a low-slung battleship-gray building in Queens called the Triboro Club. Inside, fifty men munch on six-foot hoagies and macaroni salad while inspecting row upon row of caged pigeons to be auctioned. It's a cross section of blue-collar New York: Puerto Ricans, blacks, Poles, Italians, and other eastern European and Caribbean nationals all milling around, trading breeding tips and pigeon gossip. Skin color is not an issue here; breeding winners is.

Although the Mafia's presence isn't necessarily felt, it's no secret that its members enjoy pigeon racing as well.

Reputed Genovese crime captain Anthony Federici was arrested several years ago for climbing onto the roof of his popular Queens restaurant and shooting his shotgun at hawks circling near his pigeon coop. Be that as it may, the guys here today are mostly plumbers, carpenters, and mechanics.

Today's gossip revolves around one breeder who won a series of big races the year before. Several folks suspect he drugged his birds—performance-enhancing steroids are not uncommon. Few are impressed with the birds the breeder has put up for auction. "You don't have to be a rocket scientist to see something's wrong with these birds," says John Ferarro, pointing to a shit-covered pigeon and his three shivering pals. "They're not even getting proper nutrition."

An auctioneer stands on a folding table and starts the bidding with a healthy-looking pair of gray-and-white homers. "This pair comes from Johnny Russo. Need I say more? He flies a dynamic bird. Do I hear fifty dollars? Okay, fifty-five? Sixty? Seventy? Eighty. Sold for eighty!"

Another set of birds is placed atop the makeshift podium. They waddle to the edge of the cage and stare blankly into the audience. "This man's got the finest birds around. You can't beat Don Pepe's pigeons. These birds are incredible. Do I hear a hundred? One-twenty-five? Okay, let's stop the B.S. . . . I want one-thirty . . . Sold to Ralphy!" Ralphy wears jeans, a union cap, and a Jets jacket. He retrieves the birds, holding them upside down by their feet, and walks away proudly.

"All right, fellas, listen close. These next birds are from John the Greek. We all know what kind of bird he flies. Now, this is one nice pigeon. You won't be sorry. Do I hear sixty?"

Orlando loses interest in the auction. He raises his own pigeons and often gives away his extras for free. He's here to gossip and trade tips. He gets up and walks around the perimeter of the room, inspecting the birds. "What's most important at this age is their health," he says. "You look at the droppings in the cage, making sure they're solid and not too green—that can mean salmonella or E. coli. You can smell when something's not right. You know what you feed them, so you know what should be coming out. These over here probably come from a dirty coop . . . A coop should be vacuumed once a day, minimum, and the water cans should be bleached weekly."

It's a rare moment of undistracted discourse with Orlando. Usually, he fidgets with boredom and interrupts when I ask him to explain the basics of pigeon racing. Other times he fidgets for no apparent reason. Regardless, the interviews are inevitably disrupted by the constant ringing of his cell phone. Whenever I ask what he considers a stupid or repetitive question, I'm treated to a small repertoire of expressions for impatience and frustration: "I've already explained that to you"; "It's too complicated"; and my personal favorite, "Don't make me kill again."

Orlando continues down the wall of pigeon cages. "A healthy bird should never have shit on his feet. That bird over there, he's slouched over too much. He's probably got a weak back. He's not a winner. This guy over here, his legs are too far apart. Remember, they're essentially landing gear."

He reaches into a cage, picks up a bird, and spreads one of its wings. "You always got to look at the tips of the feathers. They're like the rings in a tree. You can tell if a bird missed a day of feeding or if it didn't get enough water. Look here. You see that little line across the top? I'll bet you he was a little sick that day." A missed day of feeding, and it shows up on a feather like a ring on a tree? It's hard to tell if Orlando is a shrewd observer of all things pigeon or simply a wily bullshit artist.

Orlando opens the bird's beak and inspects for cankers and excess mucus, then holds the bird in one hand, inspecting its breastbone, or "keel," which he says should be about five fingers across. "The bird should be well proportioned. You don't want a big head or something."

Some breeders study a pigeon's eyes for pupil size and coloring, which they claim is a predictor for a bird's homing instinct. Orlando says "eye sign" is a load of crap, akin to judging an Olympic athlete by his eye color. "I'm more interested in how a bird feels in my hands and how it handles itself. He should be as curious about me as I am about him."

A bird in the next cage catches Orlando's eye. "I like that bird. Why? I wish I could tell you. Sometimes it's just the way they look at you."

A teenager approaches Orlando for advice. "My birds are sick," the boy says. "They're not dying, but they're, like, in junkie comas. Burned out. Fucked up."

Orlando quickly sums up the situation. "Give them grit, and after the grit, give them a bath and a lot of light. They should also get some acidophilus. They'll come out of it. Just don't give them antibiotics. They'll have no liver left. And they'll get immune anyway."

Orlando's fascination with pigeons dates to early childhood, shortly after his family moved to Brooklyn from Puerto Rico. "As a kid, I always looked up and watched them flying around. I just liked being around them. I still do." As young teenagers, he and José made a coop in the window of their bedroom using milk crates. "We had sixteen birds. They weren't homers; they were flights. We'd let them out the window and watch them fly in circles and come back. All the kids had them. The idea was to catch and keep another guy's bird and sell it back to him for a dollar."

A few years later, Orlando and his brother built their first rooftop loft and spent much of their time protecting it from pigeon burglars, or "tappers." "When you're living in an apartment building in the ghetto, having a coop is different," says Orlando. "The hard part is making sure no one steals your birds. We couldn't have a big coop for our flights because wood was expensive, and so the construction had to be reinforced using tar paper and tin. The coop was more like a crawl space, so no one could break in."

Before he began racing homers, Orlando used to go out drinking most nights. After a stint in jail on Rikers Island, he sobered up and rediscovered his love of pigeons. Now he's too busy with his pigeons to get in trouble. His choice of friends has changed, too. "I find myself associating mainly with other pigeon racers," he tells me. "If you tell most people you're one of the best pigeon racers in New York, they won't be impressed. But other racers? They know."

It wasn't until Orlando was in his twenties that he could actually afford his first loft of racing homers. "José and I always wanted homers, but they were beyond our reach. We were just kids. To have homers, you need a car for training and someone to guide you through it. We didn't have the knowledge, roof space, or the money."

Orlando's racing mentor was a Queens pet-shop owner by the name of Frank Klein, who learned the sport from his father. It was Klein who gave Orlando and José their first four homers. But the brothers struggled with the sport's complexity. "If we came in next to last in a race, we were happy because we weren't last," Orlando says. The next year Klein took the brothers under his wing, and OJ Loft won its first race.

"Franky saw that we had potential, that we could be contenders. He taught us everything. We were inseparable, always together. Franky's the Grand Master. There is no better. Every time I visit him, I think I should bring a tape recorder."

Klein, who's now retired and spends his time racing pigeons from his home on the Jersey shore, remembers the young Orlando as a "nice boy, a little on the wild side.

"One day Orlando comes into the store—it was called Tuttie's pet shop—and he sees my homers," Klein tells me. "He gets crazy on them. You know what I mean? He's insistent. He has to have them. He had the interest right away . . . But he didn't know anything about them. I set him straight. I got him on the right foot. You know what I'm saying?"

A few years later, in 1994, the brothers won the Main Event for the first time. "Orlando's one of the top guns in the sport right now," Klein says. "José lost interest. But Orlando? He puts the work in. You understand? It don't come from nothing. No matter how good the birds are, if you don't take care of them, nothing happens. Like racehorses. You know what I mean?"

I do know what he means. While Orlando seemingly neglects even the rudimentary tasks of daily life—such as work—he doesn't mess around with his pigeons. He cares for and trains them obsessively. To him they are little heroes capable of performing astonishing athletic feats, and they deserve to be treated accordingly.

While some might not view sports figures—avian or otherwise—as heroes, pigeons have actually saved lives, thousands of them. These intrepid birds have played a pivotal role in human history, ferrying information that helped shape the world we live in.

2

Through Rain, Sleet, and . . . a Hail of Bullets

UNTIL THE MID-NINETEENTH CENTURY, MOST INFORMATION traveled excruciatingly slowly, basically at a horse trot. But by 1850, the telegraph had altered expectations and quickly became the backbone of our information exchange. Information is, of course, a commodity. He who gets the information first has a distinct advantage over his competitors. But as nations and entrepreneurs raced to string cables across Europe, gaps in service still remained.

One man, an obscure failed German businessman by the name of Israel Beer Josaphat, had the critical insight to exploit one such gap between Brussels and Aachen, Germany. The distance was just seventy-six miles, but all the news from across France and Belgium bottlenecked at this juncture before it could once again be whisked across Germany by electrical transmission. The train between Brussels and Aachen took about eight hours, which proved a critical delay in the relay of important news and stock market prices. A pigeon could fly the distance in under two hours.

Josaphat contracted the services of an Aachen brewer who fancied pigeons, to fly his pigeons between the two cities. The news in Brussels was hung from tiny bags under the birds' wings and then flown to Aachen. The pigeons returned to the brewer's loft, where he removed the news and placed it in sealed boxes, which were then raced to an office by young boys. Josaphat, who would soon rename himself Julius Reuters in an effort to hide his Jewish origins, turned the scribbles into proper telegraphic messages and relayed them to Berlin and beyond.

Reuters didn't invent the use of pigeons to speed the transmission of information. The Rothschilds' own private pigeon post delivered news of Napoleon's defeat at Waterloo twenty-four hours before the rest of London learned of it. But for six months in 1851, after which the gap in telegraph service closed, Reuters parlayed the use of pigeons into what would become the world's largest news-gathering organization. He had created an empire literally on the backs of pigeons.

If you visit Aachen today, you might see pigeons loafing around the cathedral where Charlemagne was crowned the Holy Roman emperor in 800 A.D. But you won't see much identifying their role in early news gathering—just a small plaque on a nearby building that once served as Reuters' offices and now houses an Italian restaurant.

Although pigeons have been used as messengers in warfare since the beginning of recorded history, it wasn't until the siege of Paris during the Franco-Prussian War in 1870 that use of the rock dove entered the modern martial era. After the defeat of Emperor Napoleon III, the

31

Prussian army encircled Paris and cut off its inhabitants from the rest of France. The besieged Parisians, desperate to communicate their predicament, tried numerous ways to get messages out to their countrymen. Postal smugglers were captured and shot by the Prussians. Five sheepdog messengers were never seen again. Zinc balls filled with letters and floated down the Seine went unrecovered.

In an act of desperation, the city turned to its humblest inhabitants, and with great success. Pigeons easily carried messages from Paris to the rest of France. The use of pigeons coincided with the invention of microphotography, enabling one bird to carry as many as thirty thousand communiqués. By war's end, the birds had carried more than a million messages out of Paris.

The lesson wasn't lost on Europe's militaries, most of which established a pigeon corps of winged warriors. Their use was pivotal in World War I. As the young men of Europe set out for the muddy trenches of the Western Front, many shouldered wicker baskets filled with rock doves. Telegraph messages were often impractical during battle. The pigeon, with its 98 percent success rate, proved the most reliable way to speedily transmit critical battlefield communications. Hundreds of thousands of birds were used to deliver messages through rain and fog as well as the brutal trappings of modern warfare: barrages of artillery, poison gas, and targeted rifle fire. Twenty thousand pigeons lost their lives in combat.

Tales of pluck and valor are legion. But the story of Cher Ami is particularly memorable. Deep in the Argonne Forest, the U.S. Army's 77th Division (later known as the "Lost Battalion") was trapped behind enemy lines. In one day, heavy fighting reduced their ranks to two hundred men. Then things got even worse. Twenty-five miles away, American troops were unwittingly unleashing a massive artillery barrage on the last remnants of the battalion. With ammunition and medical supplies running low, the soldiers turned to their small flock of rock doves.

A plea for help was placed inside a canister attached to a bird's leg, and the bird was then released. The Germans spotted it, and the feathered courier was shot down before it could even orient itself above the trenches. A second bird was sent up. Once again the soldiers watched in horror as it, too, fell to earth in a cluster of blood and mangled feathers.

A third message was written: "Our artillery is dropping a barrage on us. For heaven's sake, stop it!" A soldier attached it to the third and final pigeon, a little bird by the name of Cher Ami. The soldier uncupped his hands and watched the bird flap its wings and gain altitude. The Germans also saw the pigeon and trained their rifles on it. A hail of bullets whizzed through the air and several hit Cher Ami. He quickly lost altitude and plummeted toward the ground. But moments before crashing, the bird somehow managed to spread his wings again and start climbing, higher and higher, until he was out of rifle range.

Twenty minutes later and back on friendly terrain, Cher Ami landed at headquarters. A soldier ran to the bird and found him lying on his back, covered in blood. One eye and part of the cranium had been blown away, and its breast had been ripped open. A silver canister containing the Lost Battalion's desperate plea dangled from a few tendons—all that remained of the bird's severed leg. Bewildered, the soldier rushed the message to his commanding officer. The American artillery fell silent, and the last remnants of the Lost Battalion were saved.

For his courageous persistence, Cher Ami was awarded the French Croix de Guerre. General Pershing shipped the bird back to the United States (in an officer's berth), where he received a hero's welcome. The bird died from his multiple war wounds less than a year later. His stuffed but tattered body—carefully balanced on the one remaining leg—can still be seen on display at the Smithsonian Institution in Washington, D.C.

Although technology rapidly advanced, pigeons were still a viable means of communication during World War II. After all, transmission lines can be cut and radio communications intercepted. The U.S. tripled its pigeon corps to 54,000 birds, which were trained and cared for by more than 3,000 soldiers, or "Pigeoneers."

These birds were even more carefully bred and highly trained than their World War I predecessors, able to fly much faster and twice as far. They were trained to reorient themselves to mobile lofts, fly at night, and fly with miniature cameras to take aerial reconnaissance photographs. They were secretly released from surfaced submarines to fly critical communications back to land, and parachuted from airplanes into occupied Europe. Inside each parachute harness was a message asking partisans to send back reports of enemy activity (via pigeon) to England. As dangerous as the mission might have been for the partisans, it was more perilous for the pigeons. Many were never located by partisans and remained trapped in their harnesses, fated to die an anonymous death of thirst and starvation. Others were captured by Germans and most likely eaten.

Allied forces employed pigeons across the globe, from the deserts of North Africa to the jungles of Burma. As with World War I, the number of avian heroes is too many to list. But some do stand out. A rock dove by the name of Gustav fought fierce headwinds as he flew across the English Channel to deliver first news of the D-day landings: "We are 20 miles or so off the beaches. First assault troops landed 0750. Signal says no interference from enemy gunfire on beach . . . Steaming steadily in formation . . . No enemy aircraft seen." Although feted for his historical contribution, Gustav met an inglorious end when a caretaker mucking out his loft stepped on him by accident.

Another dove by the name of Winkie escaped from a downed British bomber after the plane crashed into the North Sea. Although covered in aircraft oil, Winkie managed to fly 130 nighttime miles to Scotland with the stranded crew's coordinates tied to his ankle.

Perhaps the most famous pigeon of World War II was G.I. Joe, credited with saving the lives of more than a thousand British soldiers in October 1943. When a British brigade attacked and won back the Italian city of Colvi Vecchia from the Germans ahead of schedule, they were unable to call off a planned American air raid by radio. As a last resort, the soldiers cast a glance at the wicker basket they had carried into battle. Inside, G.I. Joe waddled about pecking for food and staring around blankly at the harried soldiers. Roused from his habitual reverie by an anxious hand, Joe waited patiently in the soldier's fist as a message was affixed to his leg. Moments later, he was tossed into the sky. The soldiers watched with a mixture of disbelief, hope, and trepidation. Once again the fate of hundreds of men rested upon the wings of a small pigeon.

Joe arrived at the American air base mere minutes before pilots took off to unwittingly bomb their British compatriots. For his gallantry, the lord mayor of London awarded G.I. Joe the prestigious Dickin Medal, the animal equivalent of the Victoria Cross. G.I. Joe was allowed to retire in style at the army's Pigeon Hall of Fame, in Fort Monmouth, New Jersey, where he lived to be an elderly eighteen years old. His feathered remains are mounted in a glass display case at the fort's museum.

The Nazis were well acquainted with the use of pigeons as well. Heinrich Himmler, a former chicken breeder, was also an avowed pigeon fancier. After the Nazi Party assumed power, Himmler declared himself head of the German National Pigeon Society and seized control of the nation's private pigeon lofts, confiscating the best racing birds in preparation for war. German spies used the birds to send secret messages back to Germany. The English, however, had some success deploying peregrine falcons, a natural predator of pigeons, to intercept the clandestine communiqués.

Occasionally, the Germans intercepted Allied pigeons as well, as was the case with a bird by the name of Lucia di Lammermoor. She was captured by German troops in 1944 in the central Italian town of Cassino. A day later, she returned to the Allied forces with a message: To the American troops, herewith we return a pigeon to you. We have enough to eat. When the Allied Forces began rolling across Germany, the Army instructed its Pigeoneers to seek out and destroy the German homing pigeon population. I spoke to one veteran who explained to me how he circumvented the order.

"When we went to see the German birds, we were stunned," says Stanley Mehr. "They were magnificent. We were poor immigrant kids from places like Brooklyn; a lot of us had never seen thoroughbreds like these. The stature, the bearing, the appearance; we knew these were premier-quality birds. We were in awe of them. The last thing we would have done is kill them.

"We came up with a better idea. We procured some scissors and clipped one wing feather off each bird—the one that's responsible for flight. It didn't harm the bird in anyway. We figured the war would be over in six months, and by that time, the feather would grow back."

The behavioral psychologist B. F. Skinner stumbled upon a rather unique use for pigeons during World War II. He taught his pigeons, which he kept in a backyard dovecote, to work as primitive missile guidance systems by pecking at a video screen with crosshairs. Although preliminary trials were relatively successful, "Project Pigeon" was a hard sell to the military. The Pentagon found the endeavor more bird-brained than practical, much like Skinner's efforts to teach his pigeons to play a crude form of Ping-Pong using their wings as paddles.

Years later, the Coast Guard experimented with pigeons on search-and-rescue missions, an avian equivalent of the time-honored canine function. The pigeons were placed in helicopters alongside human spotters and trained to identify orange life vests adrift at sea. Because of their vastly superior vision and unusual ability to concentrate for long periods of time on visual tasks—boredom doesn't fatigue pigeons—the birds outperformed their human counterparts by a margin of three to one. Although the birds were willing to work for birdseed, officials once again had difficulty taking the birds seriously, and the program was abandoned.

Many scientists remained in awe of the bird's uncanny ability to recognize visual patterns. They continued to train pigeons to perform important tasks, such as scanning airport baggage for security violations and spotting defective drug capsules on a manufacturer's assembly line. These projects, too, were met with skepticism.

Yet intelligence agencies continued to explore uses for the rock dove. According to recently declassified files from the Cold War years, the British military briefly considered arming pigeons with biological weapons. The plan was to attach small explosive capsules containing biological agents to a thousand pigeons and unleash them on the enemy. The CIA also made use of pigeons for clandestine operations, and even today the agency's Web site includes several child-friendly pages featuring a gleeful sibling spy team of pigeons: "Hi, kids! I'm Harry Recon, and this is my twin sister, Aerial . . . My family has always supported the Agency . . . We love being up in the air because it's so much fun and we take great pictures from up there as well. We love flying so much that Mom has a hard time keeping us on the ground to do our homework and our chores!"

With their use dwindling after World War II, the United States Army officially closed its pigeon courier program in 1957. Other countries such as China, France, and Spain continued to use them as messengers as the pigeon's method of delivery remains impervious to modern eavesdropping devices. American military use of pigeons surfaced again during the Gulf war and the Iraqi war, with the rock dove serving as the proverbial canary in a coal mine, accompanying troops as an early-warning sign of a chemical attack. It is rumored that Saddam Hussein relied on pigeon couriers after the U.S. tapped in to—and then decimated—his modern communication capabilities. Several stories have surfaced of army personnel finding flocks of homing pigeons in abandoned Iraqi bunkers. Their use continues well into the U.S. occupation, as Iraqi insurgents rely heavily on pigeons to ferry clandestine information.

As their use in guerrilla warfare continues to rise, so does their involvement in smuggling operations. Pigeons have been used to smuggle cocaine, heroin, and marijuana from Bogotá, Bangkok, and Berlin. Workers in South Africa diamond mines have used rock doves to sneak out rough-cut gems for sale on the black market. They taped diamonds onto the birds' legs and chests and watched them fly home.

Given the bird's innate athletic and navigational abilities, one might think that all fanciers would concentrate on these attributes. To my surprise, I found an entire subculture devoted to nothing more than the bird's looks, which they parade at annual pigeon pageants. I decided to attend but feared that it had all the makings of a shallow pursuit. It was, however, far more than that, and it opened my eyes to a fanciful and improbable world hiding in plain sight.

3

Drs. Frankenstein

THE WESTMINSTER KENNEL CLUB DOG SHOW IS THE PIN-nacle of dog shows and attracts animal lovers from every-where. Founded in 1877 and held every subsequent year at Madison Square Garden, the show outdates every other annual American sporting contest with the exception of that other princely competition, the Kentucky Derby.

Over the years, the show has attracted the attention of the world's most powerful men: J. P. Morgan entered his collies in the competition, and both the tsar of Russia and the German kaiser entered Siberian wolfhounds. In 1938, the Westminster made the cover of *Time* magazine. Today it is attended by tens of thousands of spectators and shown live on national television to millions more.

The pigeon world's equivalent, the Grand Nationals, attracts fewer than a hundred spectators and isn't televised. The media generally ignored the eighty-third Grand Nationals, which were held at a hotel in Lancaster, Pennsylvania, with its own convention space. The local newspaper covered the cattle competition at the Pennsylvania Farm Show in Harrisburg ("Maybe the drool overflowing below Vinnie the bull's nose ring turned off the judge . . .") and even the postponement of a planned poisoning of local crows. But there was no mention of the bird show.

Pigeons may have helped Noah find land. They may have saved thousands of lives during the two world wars. And they may be remarkable athletes with the homing abilities of a GPS satellite. Yet most people still consider them feathered rats. They have little interest in admiring the best efforts of champion breeders, who have spent years—often decades—patiently perfecting their pigeon stock.

These breeders represent an entirely different subculture of obsessed pigeon people. Although competitive, they have little in common with the likes of Orlando and his racing pals. For them, it has nothing to do with athletic performance or gambling; rather, it is about the dogged pursuit of a perceived platonic ideal through the painstaking application of genetic manipulation. Some of these fanciers have traveled to remote corners of the world in search of exotic breed stock to give themselves a competitive edge. Conversely, the Grand Nationals is partially filled with Middle Easterners and Asians shopping for genes.

I arrive in Pennsylvania Dutch country on a cold winter's day and check in to a motel across the street from the pageant. I am lucky to find a room on short notice, given that more than five hundred pigeon breeders and their families have planned for a year to inundate the area.

Once inside the hotel hosting the pageant, I veer across the lobby and head for the exhibit hall. Before me is a room, nearly the size of a football field, stacked with thousands of pigeons. Row upon row of cooing, pooing pigeons. I count twenty-four rows of large folding wooden exhibition tables, each double lined with double stacks—more than twenty-five hundred birds, each in its own cage with its own colorful Dixie cups of feed and water and red rosin paper flooring. I soon learn that there's another show arena, the hotel's twenty-five-thousand-square-foot expo center, stacked with *twice* as many birds and breeders.

The exhibit hall cackles with excited breeders attending to their avian dependents and greeting fellow hobbyists in warm fellowship. Wafting around the lights is a dusty haze of fine particles containing the deeply organic smell of birdseed, bird droppings, and molting feathers. Breeders move about the cages in white lab coats designed to protect their clothes from bird droppings and the hovering particulate matter. Some wear surgical masks to protect their lungs.

I have never seen so many birds in one place. It is as if someone has taken all the birds from Venice's St. Mark's Square and placed them indoors. But one thing is decidedly different: There are no ordinary street pigeons here. These pigeons are some of the strangest-looking feathered beasts I've ever witnessed.

There are pigeons with giant fanned tails much like a turkey's, pigeons with beaks so small they have difficulty eating, and others whose throats extend into balloons the size of grapefruits. Some have feathers that curl like corkscrews, while still others have giant feathers jutting out from their feet like Oriental fans. There are dozens of breeds of pigeon, each grouped by club so members can compete against one another for Best of Breed. Unlike at Westminster, however, there is no climactic Best in Show category. (Nor, for that matter, is there a central staging area where breeders trot in circles before a large audience with their pigeons on leashes.)

The caged pigeons come in a multitude of sizes, from the curiously named giant runt, which is the size of an oven roaster, to the palm-sized pygmies. And they come in a multitude of colors and hues: whites, browns, blacks, blues, grays, and iridescent purples, reds, and pinks, some spotted, others speckled or striped.

One gentleman stands out from the rest of the breeders. He's wearing fashionably thick black glasses and slick metro wear—black jeans, boots, and blazer. Steve Gaskin is a hairdresser and a breeder of Jacobins from Dallas, Texas. He's attending the conference with Bonnie, a coworker and friend for twenty years. The pair met when Bonnie was interviewed at his salon wearing nothing but leggings, a sweater, and big red boots. "I just *had* to hire her!" Gaskin recalls. "Can you imagine that outfit?"

Growing up in rural Arkansas, Gaskin bred all sorts of animals. "I had quarter horses, peacocks, monkeys, you name it. My parents were *very* indulgent." But it was the pigeons, Jacobins in particular, that caught his eye as soon as he was old enough to hightail it out of cotton country. "I left as soon as I could drive. My family had been there for generations, but the country life wasn't for me. Even my mother told me so. She said, 'Steve, this isn't for you.' Now I live in the city, in Dallas proper."

They say breeding pigeons is an art form, a perfect blend of beauty and form. If that's the case, then Jacobins are surely the work of masters. In the world of pigeons, they are perhaps the most extravagantly stylish breed. Jacobins are also one of the oldest breeds, tracing back over a thousand years to India. They are believed to have made their way to Europe by way of Cyprus, birthplace of Aphrodite. The birds have delicate bodies with rich, dense feathering. Their most distinctive feature is their reverse-feathered hood. From a distance, their heads look as if they've been replaced with pom-poms. On closer inspection, you see that the head is completely surrounded by a regal-looking mane of soft feathers, like Greta Garbo snuggled in a fur coat. It is said that England's Queen Elizabeth I was particularly fond of breeding them and that they may have been the inspiration for her outlandishly high collars. The effect comes from feathers around the neck that are naturally reversed. They point toward the head and the sky instead of resting smoothly on the back and pointing toward the tail.

Gaskin's flock is in a handful of cages around all the other Jacobins. He points out his birds' droppings. They look like hard little balls on the rosin paper. It means his birds are healthy, he says. A splattered green crap means illness.

"My birds aren't necessarily winners, but I've got some pretty good birds. Like this one, he's pretty good." Gaskin taps his finger against a cage, and a hooded pigeon scurries to the other side. "And this one is pretty good, too. But come over here. These are exquisite!" Gaskin approaches a nationally famous breeder of Jacobins and his birds. "Hi. I'm Steve Gaskin, from Dallas, and I just noticed your birds. They are beautiful, beautiful birds. Would you be willing to sell me one?"

"No."

"Well, I had to ask!" Gaskin walks back to his birds. "His are the best, but he never wants to sell. Jacobins are so hard to breed that most breeders won't sell."

He stops to point out a few more exemplary Jacobins. "Why do I like this one?" he asks rhetorically, singling out an elegant bird. "Number one, his station. And his neck feathers stand up nicely." He moves on to another bird. "This one here has a slight imperfection. It's called 'shingling'—a feather falls down instead of sitting upright. The competition doesn't allow gels or trimming. If there's a flaw, it will show, and you just have to live with it."

Farther down the exhibition hall is Larry Reifsnyder, a fifty-six-year-old carpenter from nearby Reading, Pennsylvania. His pigeon club is sponsoring the event. He spent the previous Sunday setting up hundreds of tables and thousands of cages with the help of a Boy Scout troop. "Our club is getting older and smaller these days, so we need the help—there's just nine of us. The older guys are dying, and there aren't any new youngsters joining. We can't put on a show like this without help."

Although the convention hall is full, the average age is probably in the mid-fifties. "Kids today want instant gratification, and pigeons take too long," Reifsnyder says. "Used to be everything revolved around the backyard— your fraternal lodge backyard, your church backyard, your own backyard where you kept pigeons. These days zoning ordinances make it difficult to do anything in your backyard. But in the day, you bred pigeons in your backyard, and they were your life . . . People just don't join clubs anymore. Hobbyists are a dying breed. Nowadays all kids want to do is hang out at the mall, watch movies, watch television, and play Nintendo. And yet they're still bored. Imagine that."

Like many of the fanciers, Reifsnyder started breeding pigeons as a youngster and stopped for a dozen years or so after he discovered girls, only to start up again as an escape from the stresses of family life. "Breeding gives me pleasure. It's a diversion from what I'd ordinarily be doing. It's satisfying to start with a pair of birds, mate them, and then see how the babies turn out. It's a lot of work, but it's also relaxing." Reifsnyder's ex-wife was less enthusiastic about the hobby. "She'd say to me, 'You just like manipulating birds, that's why you like it.' Well, in a sense she was right, that's why we all do it—to see what we can get out of our birds."

Reifsnyder raises Oriental frills, a pigeon with a pronounced forehead and minuscule pug-nosed beak. Like the Jacobins, the Oriental frills have reversed feathering, but theirs is small and located on their upper chests, resembling a European cravat. They also have a handful of feathers that stick up on the back of their heads and give their skulls a crest. The birds' mouths are so misshapen that they have to eat out of a cup; their beaks are too small to peck at the ground. Nor can they feed their babies, which, incidentally, can't even peck their way out of their shells. These basic biological tasks are left to the breeder.

"The better ones have a harder time eating because they have less beak," says Reifsnyder. "They certainly wouldn't survive in the wild, but then again, they're not bred to live in the wild. They're bred to be pretty to look at."

To me they all look brown and white. But Reifsnyder points out subtleties of color with racy names like "Blondette" and "Black Lace Satin." I may be daft or color blind, but they all still look the same to me. Reifsnyder points to a Black Lace Blonde that looks more like a brunette to me. "This is a real good one. See how she has a full head and how it rolls back real well, too?"

He picks up another bird, cups it in his hand, and effortlessly flicks open its wing as if it were a cigarette lighter. "See the edging around the feathers? If you look real close, it's a bit smutty, blurry. What you want is a good white background and a darker, vivid outline."

He hands the bird to me, and I grasp it awkwardly. I can feel the bird's heart beating furiously. "He doesn't much like being held. This one's always been nervous. He tries to hide in the corner from the judge. It's a shame, because he's got excellent traits, and that's what he's supposed to do—show them off.

"I've worked with numerous breeds—English trumpeters, Russian trumpeters, Lahores, magpies, tumblers, pouters. I don't know why I stuck with Oriental Frills. Why do you like a certain girl? She just catches your eye . . . They're a stupid but generally calm breed. If you let them out of their cage, they can't even find their way home. Whatever direction they start out in, they just keep heading in that direction. But I really like this breed's colors and color patterns. I like the lace pattern. Oh yeah, I really like the lace. If Jacobins had lace, I'd probably raise them. But it could take a lifetime to inject a stencil pattern into that breed. It's really hit-and-miss."

I remain perplexed. Why pigeons? He says, "Why do people like dogs? I'm not particularly fond of dogs.

I guess I like pigeons because they're pretty. Actually, that's a good question. I never really thought about it. Honestly."

He selects another bird. "This one has a nice wide head, but there's a break in its mane. Its head is crested, but it's not needle-pointed. That's a point reduction, but it's not a disqualification. It could still win if there's not a better young cock. But put it up against an old cock, and it'll probably lose because he'll have more powerful frills. Frills don't fully mature until two to three years of age. Now, if you have a young cock that beats an old cock, well, that's one hell of a cock." Reifsnyder shakes his head knowingly. Even the thought of such a bird leaves him speechless.

Cocks, as you might suspect, are male birds. A young cock is any cock under the age of one. All the rest are old cocks. Female birds, or hens, are classified similarly. Reifsnyder says, "I'd rather win with a hen than a cock because it's harder. And hens are the key to breeding anyway. Cocks just give color. Hens pass on type and power." "Type" is the way the carriage is formed and how the bird stands. "Most of the points in this breed are in the nose; that's where the power is. It's like a bull's-eye area . . . But the fact is, you'll never have a perfect bird."

Reifsynder suggests that I seek out a gentleman in the expo center who goes by the moniker "Dr. Pigeon." "He knows a heck of a lot more than me. He's a walking encyclopedia about pigeons."

Befriending Dr. Pigeon, I soon learn, will help open doors for me that I otherwise would have found slammed in my face. Dr. Pigeon has clout, particularly in the shady underworld of live pigeon shoots.

But before meeting more breeders, I want more background on just what's going on around me. I need to reacquaint myself with two guys I haven't thought about since high school—Darwin and Mendel. Only then will I get a clear picture of how breeders think and work.

4

Evolution, Peapods, and Pigeons

Believing that it is always best to study some special group, I have joined two of the London Pigeon Clubs. The diversity of the breeds is something astonishing . . . Such are the variations that an ornithologist would certainly rank them as well-defined species. Yet I am fully convinced that the common opinion of naturalists is correct, namely, that all have descended from the wild rock-pigeon (Columba livia).
—Charles Darwin, *The Origin of Species*

THE GALÁPAGOS ISLANDS ARE A SMALL VOLCANIC ARCHI-pelago about six hundred miles west of Ecuador. The oldest islands are several million years old, and the youngest are still being formed by lava flows. The first recorded sighting of the islands was by the bishop of Panama, whose boat was blown off course in 1535. For hundreds of years afterward, the islands were rarely visited, except by pirate vessels and whaling ships.

The young naturalist Charles Darwin would make them famous following his monthlong sojourn there in 1835. It wasn't the harsh geography that seduced Darwin. "Nothing could be less inviting," he wrote in *Voyage of the Beagle,* describing the islands as "a broken field of black basaltic lava, thrown in the most rugged waves, and crossed by great fissures." What attracted Darwin was the remoteness of the islands and their uncommon animal inhabitants.

Born into a well-to-do British family in 1809, Darwin rarely excelled at his studies and was an academic disappointment to his father. He was first sent to the University of Edinburgh to study medicine. When that didn't pan out, Darwin transferred to Cambridge University with the intention of becoming a clergyman. But Darwin soon fell under the spell of a natural sciences professor who recommended him for the position of naturalist on the H.M.S. *Beagle.* Prone to seasickness, Darwin spent much of the two-year voyage nauseated and, once home, never set foot on another oceangoing vessel.

As he surveyed the Galápagos Islands, Darwin was repeatedly struck by the variations among seemingly similar species. Not only did the animals vary from known species on the west coast of South America, they differed from island to island. As Darwin sailed around the archipelago, he identified thirteen different species of finches alone. The greatest physical variation was in the bird's beak. Some finches had developed long, slender bills to extract pulp from a prickly pear cactus. Some had large beaks for cracking hard seeds. Others had small, thin beaks for extracting grubs.

Darwin surmised that the finches had somehow made their way to the Galápagos from the mainland and had developed different physical attributes over time. He hypothesized that the birds had adapted different beak characteristics to better exploit their food source. Darwin was relatively certain these birds had evolved, but it would take several more years to develop his thinking. His writings about the Galápagos tentatively speculated about evolution but did not address how it occurred.

Darwin did not invent the theory of evolution. Fossil evidence had already cast doubt on the creation myth of Genesis. Darwin's great contributions would be the how and why of evolution. And it wasn't the Galápagos and its finches that led him to his theory of natural selection. In fact, he rarely addressed either of them again. Instead, it was his work with pigeons that focused his thinking and sharpened his arguments.

The theory of natural selection maintains that animals will adapt over time to survive better in their environment. Those who are better adapted will thrive and pass on their traits to successive generations. The healthy will leave more descendants than the unhealthy.

Natural selection occurs over huge expanses of time. In today's world, we can witness it happening more rapidly, such as with antibiotic-resistant bacteria. Darwin didn't have the luxury of modern microbiology. But while he may not have been able to see natural selection at work in the wild, Darwin suspected he could see it under controlled conditions with the breeding of domestic pigeons, thereby imitating in years what occurs in nature over eons.

Darwin soon filled his backyard with fancy pigeons from around the world and set to work breeding them. In time, he was convinced that although some of the birds had large fanned tails, and others strangely feathered feet, they all shared a common ancestor, *Columba livia*—the humble rock dove. Darwin speculated (correctly) that if the different fancy breeds were allowed to mate freely in the wild, the offspring would eventually lose their distinctive traits and resemble the rock dove. Darwin termed this phenomenon "reversion."

In Darwin's time, it was generally believed, even by breeders, that each fanciful breed of pigeon was a separate species with little or nothing in common. "I have never met a pigeon fancier who was not fully convinced that each main breed was descended from a distinct species," wrote Darwin in *The Origin of Species*. "When I first kept pigeons and watched the several kinds, well knowing how truly they breed, I felt fully as much difficulty in believing that, since they had been domesticated, they had all proceeded from a common parent . . . in nature."

Reversion was a revolutionary idea, one that many breeders still marvel at today. Could all their unusual and weird-looking birds really be descendants of one bird—the rock dove?

Difficult to imagine, perhaps, but as Darwin argued in *The Origin of Species*—he devoted the whole first chapter to the domestication of pigeons—there is no other reasonable explanation for the profusion of fancy pigeons. If they all came from separate stock, then where is the aboriginal stock? Why have they not been identified anywhere in the known world? And why, unlike the rock dove, are there no feral fantails or pouters? Why is it that when two birds of distinct breeds and colors are crossed, their offspring show the markings and coloration of an ordinary rock dove?

As Darwin noted, pigeons have been bred for fanciful characteristics since the beginning of recorded history: "It is in human nature to value any novelty, however slight, in one's own possession." The Roman historian Pliny observed that his countrymen paid exorbitant prices for pigeons with good pedigrees. They were also favorites of early Persian monarchs and the khans of India.

So how did a distinct breed such as the Jacobin first occur? Someone probably found a pigeon with an odd mutation—a reversed feather—and liked it (humans, after all, are rarely satisfied with the status quo). That breeder then bred the trait into his flock to intensify it. Over time the Jacobin breed was born and has been continually refined, even to this day: evolution of the man-made variety. Take the modern racing homer, a cross of eight different breeds, all of which contribute to its uncanny athletic and homing ability.

Living organisms, therefore, are not static but malleable. Species are not created out of whole cloth, as the Bible would have us believe, but rather they evolved over time through selective breeding. The mechanism in charge of driving this evolution is natural selection. While man uses unnatural selection to breed pigeons for whimsy— pigeons that would not survive in the wild—nature uses *natural* selection to ensure that the fittest survive. Variation in the wild is a necessity. It allows for adaptation, which in turn encourages survival.

After twenty years of anguished self-editing, Darwin finally published *The Origin of Species* in 1859. Darwin's editor remained skeptical of the level of interest in such a theory and encouraged him to write his next book solely about pigeons, which were a popular topic of the day. However, the first printing of *Origin* sold out the day of its release. Humanity's view of its place in the world would be forever changed.

Darwin, who belonged to two London pigeon breeding clubs, continued to pursue his beloved hobby. In 1868 he published his treatise *The Variation of Animals and Plants Under Domestication,* which included an exhaustive survey of pigeons. In it, Darwin laid out his theory of inheritance, the mechanism by which selected traits were passed down to succeeding generations.

Although Darwin had correctly surmised that some traits were dominant over others, his early forays into what would become genetics were greatly flawed. He suggested that traits were inherited through a process he named "pangenesis." Each cell in the body released tiny particles, he argued, that combined in the sexual organs to make eggs and sperm. During conception, these traits would mix and result in offspring that were a blended dilution of their parents.

Strangely enough, Darwin was contradicting his own theory of natural selection. According to pangenesis, any new trait that aided in a species' survival would be blended out of existence in a short period of time. Reconciliation of the two theories would come later, with the help of an Austrian monk.

As Darwin was publishing his *Origin of Species,* a mild-mannered monk in a secluded monastery a thousand miles away was also addressing the mysteries of heredity. It was his research that would untangle Darwin's dilemma and restore natural selection to its central role in evolutionary theory.

(Gregor) Johann Mendel was born in 1822 to peasant farmers in what was then a rural region of Austria. A sickly child with no obvious aptitude for agriculture, Mendel excelled at his school studies. His family scraped together what little they had—including his sister's future dowry—to send Mendel to preparatory school. He thrived there and was admitted to university, but a lack of finances forced him to drop out after his first year.

Left with few options to pursue his education, Mendel joined an Augustinian monastery that encouraged higher learning and scientific experimentation. Mendel was given the monastic name Gregor and remained at the St. Thomas Monastery for the rest of his life.

He was assigned to a secondary school, where he was a popular teacher. However, after failing the state examination for teacher certification, he was sent to the University of Vienna to prepare to take it again. There, Mendel acquired the research skills that he would apply to understanding heredity. Two years later, Mendel once again failed the examination, allegedly due to a case of nerves.

Although he continued to teach part-time, Mendel refocused his energies on the mystery of heredity, taking a particular interest in pea plants. Over a period of seven years, he planted nearly thirty thousand of them. Like pigeons, pea plants are relatively straightforward to work with. Mendel selected twenty-two varieties of peas and interbred them, keeping track of seven distinct traits, such as seed texture (smooth or wrinkled) and flower color (white or purple).

The results suggested that the theory of blending and dilution was hopelessly inaccurate. When Mendel bred a tall pea plant with a short one, the result was not a plant of medium height; the hybrid offspring were all tall. Mendel deduced that the trait for tallness was somehow dominant over the trait for shortness. He also noticed that if he created hybrids of the new tall plants, the result was a mix of tall and short plants. Even more intriguing, the ratio of small to large plants was mathematically predictable— a three-to-one ratio. Breeding wasn't haphazard: *It followed a predictable pattern.*

Darwin may have been correct in his assumption that some kind of code was passed from one generation to the next, but as Mendel proved, they did not blend. The codes—what we now call genes—remained intact. Some of these codes may absent themselves in one generation only to reappear in another: The genetic material was merely in recessive hiding. By negating the premise of blending, the Catholic monk also breathed new life into Darwin's theory of natural selection and restored it to its central role in evolution.

After eight years of meticulous and painstaking work, Mendel presented his theory to the local society of natural scientists. It was received with polite silence. Nobody in the room understood the importance of Mendel's groundbreaking discovery. A year later, Mendel's research appeared in the society's small journal, where it languished in obscurity.

In desperation, Mendel mailed out forty reprints of his paper to prominent scientists throughout Europe. Although the story may be apocryphal, it is thought that Darwin received a copy but never bothered to read it. He wasn't the only one. It was an uphill battle, an unknown author writing in an unknown journal. Mendel received only one reply, from a well-respected German botanist. The botanist must have merely glanced at the findings, which included data from tens of thousands of plants, because he labeled Mendel's work "incomplete" and suggested that the monk continue his research with hawkweed.

The result proved a disaster because hawkweed, as botanists would later learn, reproduces asexually. The data was inconclusive and filled Mendel with self-doubt. Discouraged, Mendel concentrated on other, nonscientific matters. In 1868 he was elected the monastery's abbot and spent many of his last sixteen years embroiled in a bitter dispute with the government over taxation of the monastery. It would be several more decades before the humble monk's work was rediscovered and universally embraced.

An early-twentieth-century English geneticist named Reginald Punnett would later develop a graphical way to calculate the mathematical probability of inheriting a specific trait. The Punnett square looks like a tic-tac-toe board. Maybe you experimented with it in high school biology class while pondering who would make use of such a thing.

Rest assured that nearly every breeder at the Grand Nationals is intimately acquainted with the graphic representation of Mendel's theory. Before Mendel and Punnett, breeders would just mate a bunch of birds together and cross their fingers. It was basically guessing.

Take color, for instance. Pigeon fanciers love to manipulate their birds' colors. Granted, pigeons are not as brilliantly colored as parrots; indeed, they may look bland and muddy-colored to most of us. But to a trained eye, their colorings are all distinct, sometimes even bewitching.

Pigeons come in three basic colors: blue, ash red, and brown. Blue bar and blue checkered are dominant, which explains why wild pigeons—the ones you see in the park—generally have that coloring; it's the original color of the rock dove. "Blue bar" means that the bird is a slate-blue-gray with two black bars, or narrow strips of color, across each wing and one bar of white on the tail. "Checkered" means that instead of bars, the pigeons have spots on their wings and tails. Other modifiers include "dilute" (for dilution of color), "lace" (Reifsnyder's favorite pattern), "saddle mark," "dominant opal," "frill," "indigo," and on and on. Add up all these colors, their variations, and the legion of color modifiers, let alone their combinations, and, as you can see, the coloration possibilities for a pigeon are nearly infinite—we're talking about complicated Punnett calculations.

Manipulating these colors for the sake of beauty is a challenging proposition. For each color, there are well over a dozen color modifiers, genes that modify the pigment in some way, shape, or form. These modifiers can also be packed one on top of another. For instance, you can have a pigeon with blue bar coloring as well as several modifiers, such as "grizzle" (in which the black bar speckling extends to the rest of the bird) and "spread" (in which the black bar color spreads in a more uniform manner so that whole sections of the bird are black).

On the first day of the pageant, I met a breeder named Andrew Kerns, a thirty-year-old beverage salesman from suburban Virginia who is embarking on a thirteen-year project to "paint" delicately stenciled wing bars onto the feathers of the fantail breed. At the time, his explanation of hereditary traits and the pigeon genome flew right over my head.

I was not alone in my confusion. Even aficionados compare breeding for a specific trait, such as color, to painting with invisible ink: You don't know what your work will look like until it's done. But backyard geneticists such as Kerns are persistent, driven by a combination of scientific hubris and a competitive nature. "I want to do something that has never been done. I'm introducing a color into this breed that wasn't there before. You can't find a fantail with this coloring anywhere. So I'm going to make it from scratch."

First, Kerns mated his fantails to a Modena pigeon with the stenciled markings. Modenas don't look anything like fantails—they have short tails, large heads, and thick, meaty horizontal bodies. Kerns ended up with "a bunch of really odd-looking Modenas with extra tail feathers." Toying with nature—and thousands of years of genetic evolution—is a painfully difficult process, even for an expert like Kerns. "It's one step forward to keep the type and a half-step backwards to keep the color," he tells me. "You lose the color every time you don't mate it with another bird with the same color. Most people would have said 'screw it' by now."

Armed with some basic genetic knowledge, I now understand what these breeders are up to. But I'm still left unprepared when it comes to meeting Dr. Pigeon, a giant among his peers and my conduit into the brutal underworld of "pigeon sport."

5

Dr. Pigeon, I Presume?

EARLY THE NEXT MORNING THE FLOOR IS ALREADY HUMMING loudly with activity, the floors littered once again with feathers and feed. I'm surprised when a pimpled teenager training to be a security guard at the local vocational school stops me on my way in and asks to search my backpack. He then describes the weekend's patrol procedures—no bird may come or go from Friday at seven A.M. to Saturday at five P.M., and it's lights out for the pigeons at eleven P.M. The expo is emptied of people, and the doors are all secured.

"Basically my job during the day is to watch what comes and goes," the guard tells me. "I don't want a bag coming in empty leaving full." His radio squawks, and he responds with an "affirmative" followed by "ten-four," then goes back to carefully scanning the pigeon area for any unusual activity.

On the ground floor, vendor booths are filled with a plethora of pigeon products. There are tables with avian medications, advanced watering systems, and an assortment of hoes and hand scrapers for cleaning bird shit off a loft floor. The selection of protein and vitamin blends, with names like Hemoglobal and Victory Pills, wouldn't look out of place in a gym.

Several tables display artwork by painters whose specialty is pigeons: pigeons in flight or a handsome specimen of a breed at rest on a perch. There is also a booth that will photograph your pigeon and transfer the image onto mugs, plates, T-shirts, and tote bags. The couple who owns the booth usually work the wedding and bar mitzvah circuit and are clearly harried from working with pigeons, which struggle as they are placed into the small Plexiglas box to be photographed. "You can tell a person to stand still and smile," the woman says, "but the birds are all over the place."

I approach a vendor who runs a pigeon supply store in Connecticut. His table is filled with wooden nest eggs (for culling), particulate respirators (fancy versions of white surgical masks), vaccines, antibiotics, brewer's yeast, and race bands. There's even a selection of different stone grits to aid a pigeon's digestion. A much larger company that has been in business over a hundred years sells still more grit products across the way. One is named Grit Concentrate #676, "to be used in combination with crushed granite and oyster shells." The Connecticut vendor tells me that, while his business is on the smaller side, he still grosses over $1 million a year and expects to gross as much as $20,000 during the three-day pageant. "You can make a living," he confides.

One table over, Dean Crozom, a soft-spoken farmer from Saskatchewan, displays more than a dozen types of colorful grains and seeds. During a lull, he explains their differences. "First you have the cereal grains, the wheat, barley, corn, millet, milo, oats, and triticale. They're higher in carbs and give more energy. Remember, birds have different nutritional needs depending on whether they're racing, breeding, molting, or what have you. For each need, there's a particular feed blend. Now, these over here, they're the legumes. They're high in protein, which promotes muscle growth. We also have green peas, trapper peas, maple peas, and Austrian peas. And we have lentils. Then you have your oil seeds, like sunflower, safflower, canola, and flax. They're a good source of protein and a lot of oil, which gives birds shiny feathers. It's every bird's favorite, so I imagine it must taste good. Birds love safflower, black oil sunflower, peanuts, canola, and millet, both red and white."

I ask Dean about birdseed blends for home use. I had been using a premium mix for my own backyard, and the songbirds loved it. But then I switched to a cheaper mix—it *was* on sale—and the birds all disappeared. It took months—long lonely months of waiting—to coax them back from my neighbors' yards. It never occurred to me that songbirds could be so picky, especially with a New England winter approaching. My attempt at thrift was met with empty perches. Gone were the tufted titmice, robins, cardinals, blue jays, blackcapped chickadees, and mourning doves. Crows and squirrels filled the void. The songbirds had spoken—guilty as charged.

"Well, the *cheaper* stuff, which you used, often has a lot of barley, and barley is their least favorite," Dean says. "They don't much like milo, red or white, either. And the cracked corn and wheat are just there to make the bag look bigger when you buy it. I suggest more oil seeds and peanuts, which, of course, cost more." I take in the full meaning of his company slogan: "Because . . . only the best will do."

I drift over to the acres of birdcages. There are Saxton pouters, Old German croppers, English pouters, and pygmy pouters, to name just a few breeds in the pouter section. Most share a softball-sized crop; some inflate to the size of a bowling ball. When a crop is distended, it is big enough to completely obscure the bird's head from certain angles.

All birds have this adaptive organ, which enables them to "eat and run" at a moment's notice. (A pigeon's crop has the unusual ability to also produce milk.) Under normal conditions, the crop is a very small pouch at the base of the neck where the bird stores partially digested food before it moves on to the stomach. These birds have crops that look like enlarged goiters, only filled with air. I watch a pigeon handler pick up one of the pouters and squeeze all the air out of its crop, just for fun. The action makes a whooshing sound, as from a rapidly deflating balloon.

The English pouters strut about on particularly long roadrunner-like legs and look as if they are wearing white leggings (the kind Russell Crowe wore in *Master and Commander*). The Saxton pouters have so many long feathers radiating from their feet that they can hardly walk without tripping. It's as if someone tied Oriental fans to their ankles.

I also see Frillbacks, which are just odd enough to be strangely beautiful. They become my favorite breed of the show. Their feathers are coiled like a corkscrew, looking as if they were dipped in Jheri curl. The magpies, with giraffe-like necks, walk about awkwardly on stilt-like legs. There are birds with horizontal carriages that resemble odd-looking chickens, and others with carriages so vertical they appear to be standing erect, like a human. Some have giant nose wattles, and others have shiny iridescent feathers, making them look like walking prisms.

Out of the corner of my eye, I spot a bird prancing about with a peacock-like tail but seemingly without a head. When viewed straight on, a fantail looks like a cross between Foghorn Leghorn and the Headless Horseman of Sleepy Hollow. It has a large, broad, and nearly vertical chest with wings that hang down like arms. The body is supported on two meaty drumsticks. From the side, you can see the neck, tucked away between the shoulder blades with the head itself resting against the base of the tail. In this pose, the bird can't see forward and generally stares upward at about a 150-degree angle. It looks to be in desperate need of a chiropractor, assuming it even has neck bones. Several birds share a cage and bounce into one another like bumper cars.

And then there's the Naked Neck, a barren-necked bird that, ironically, originated in Transylvania, home of the neck-piercing Dracula. The bird has feathers on its carriage, feathers on its wings, feathers on its tail, and feathers on its head. But due to some genetic mutation that has been exaggerated through breeding, there is not one feather poking out from its chin to its breastbone. Unlike the white-headed raptor that serves as America's emblem, this bird is truly bald. It's so ugly that even champion breeders tend to shy away from it, and as a result the bird is exceedingly rare. There is just one lonely Naked Neck at the pageant.

It's then that I spot Muard Melvin MacRae Naugle, Jr., aka Dr. Pigeon, who often signs his name "M3N Jr." A short, stocky man in his late seventies, Dr. Pigeon is bursting with energy and speaks so quickly that I have to ask him to slow down so I can take notes. He is one of only three people to be named an all-breed judge by the National Pigeon Association, which means that he is qualified to judge the standards of more than three hundred unique breeds at the show. He has bred pigeons since 1935 and has been a member of the National Pigeon Association since 1941.

Dr. Pigeon tells me that he used to read Wendell Levi's famous tome, *The Pigeon,* annually since it was first published sixty years ago. Still considered by many to be the definitive resource on pigeons, the book discusses the bird's history, anatomy, breeds, behavior, and more. "I read it every year and then started again from the beginning. I read the footnotes and all. I quit after forty years. I figured I had learned it by then."

Dr. Pigeon wears a white lab coat with dozens of patches and a button that declares, I LOVE WOMEN! Unlike most breeders, who have intricately airbrushed portraits of their favorite birds painted onto the backs of their coats, Dr. Pigeon's has been left blank. "I've worked with a hundred fifty-seven breeds and thousands of birds. Which one am I supposed to paint on my back?"

Dr. Pigeon is a vegetarian and a practicing Buddhist who meditates an hour a day. He lives in a dilapidated cabin with no heat or running water and uses a chamber pot. When it's really cold, he wraps himself in aluminum foil—shiny side down works best—to stay warm. There was a time a few years ago when he lived on fifty cents a week, eating only spaghetti. He didn't have a working stove, so he soaked the dry noodles in cold water for several days until they got soft enough to eat. "Back then I sat around and did nothing. Barely left the house. I guess you could say I was depressed."

Clearly, you don't need big money to participate in the sport. "Money helps speed the process—helps you buy better birds to start out with—but you can be a poor person and be a champion. I have a lot of trophies."

Dr. Pigeon says he saves money by operating on his pigeons when necessary. He had one bird with a tumor next to its eye. Dr. Pigeon removed the eye so he could cut out the tumor and then slid the eyeball back in. Unfortunately, the eye kept falling out, so Dr. Pigeon sewed one stitch from eyelid to eyelid, and that worked. "As soon as I was done, he was pecking around like nothing happened, like the whole operation didn't mean a thing. Pigeons have an unbelievable endurance for pain. Who knows? Maybe they don't feel pain." I would hear this outlandish refrain later, when I meet Dr. Pigeon's friends, who use pigeons for live target practice.

As we walk around the convention hall, Dr. Pigeon points out several birds. One is a carrier pigeon, the genetic precursor to the homing pigeon. It's a tall bird, eighteen inches high, but its most distinguishing feature is a collection of fleshy growths around its upper and lower beak and eyelids. Dr. Pigeon picks up the bird and starts touching the bulbous wattle like a neurosurgeon poking through squishy brain matter. He points out the bird's nearly hidden nostrils. "It's not pretty, but because it's so unusual, so far from the norm, I think it's beautiful in its own way."

As we head toward the curly Frillbacks, Dr. Pigeon explains what makes one bird a winner and another a loser. "What you're looking for in this breed is curls all over, as well as the length of the curls. That's what separates the men from the boys." He extends a telescoping pointer used for judging and aims it at a bird quietly resting in the corner of its cage. "Look at that curl. It must be two inches long. This bird has a *wealth* of curl."

Even Dr. Pigeon marvels that all these fanciful breeds have one common progenitor. "All these traits, they're recessive," he tells me. "They were selected by man and constantly improved upon to fit an aesthetic ideal. And once that ideal is reached, the bar is raised again—maybe the tail should have a more acute angle, maybe a thicker neck, a bigger head, and so on. But if they're not actively maintained, these traits will all disappear. It's a constant battle to get these birds to where they are and to keep them there. It's not easy, which is why it's competitive. That's why we have shows."

I pop the question: Could he help get me into a live bird shoot? I've been told that Dr. Pigeon lives in the same small Pennsylvania town as Don Bailey, the man who supplies local gun clubs with avian fodder.

Dr. Pigeon eyes me suspiciously. "Yeah, I know Bailey. Those gun clubs are private, you understand. They got a right to do what they do. They shoot street pigeons—they're filthy, like rats, and they give our birds a bad name."

A pause. Then: "Just tell Bailey Dr. Pigeon sent ya."

With that, the "doctor" pulls a deck of cards from his pocket and wanders off to perform card tricks for fellow breeders.

Later that night, I attend a banquet where Grand National champs schmooze, accept honorary certificates and give the equivalent of awkward Oscar night speeches. The room itself is decidedly less glamorous than the Kodak

Theatre: the drop ceiling is low, the lighting poor, and the carpet a drab diamond pattern.

The men are wearing coats and ties or shirts buttoned all the way to the top. The women wear gala dresses. The room is filled with the random firing of camera flashes.

The master of ceremonies calls various breeders to the makeshift podium. Next to be honored is Sal Gigante. He's a master breeder of domestic show flights, and the National Pigeon Association wants to recognize his contribution to competitive breeding. Sal's a big guy who wears his hair slicked back and looks like a cross between three different characters on *The Sopranos*—Silvio, Paulie Walnuts, and Big Pussy.

The flight is the quintessential New York City rooftop pigeon, generally favored by poorer immigrants who can't afford homers. Until the 1950s, nobody thought to breed them for show, so there were no show standards for the bird. A group of fanciers banded together, hashed out standards, competed among themselves, and started touring the competitive circuit.

When I met Sal earlier in the day, he was chewing on a cigar stub and judging show flights. He has scowling eyebrows and what looks like a perpetual "don't fuck with me" frown. Then again, I've seen his mood quickly lighten and his big smile light up a room.

At the banquet, all traces of the scowling tough guy are gone. Sal's eyes are wet with appreciation. After years of hard work, he's at the apex of his chosen sport, and he's humbled. The room fills with applause.

"Let me first say that the honor is not in receiving this award," he says in a wavering voice. "The honor is in giving back to the community who presents the award . . ."

Back outside the banquet, I traverse the lobby and notice flashes of light emanating from a darkened side room. Inside, I find Layne Gardner, a middle-school band director from central California, sweating under bright spotlights in the cramped and airless room while he diligently photographs the two hundred best-of-breeds. He has constructed a five-sided white box where he poses each champion "just right," using a pointer to coax the birds into a proper quarter-turn pose. It looks like a lonesome and frustrating pursuit, not to mention uncomfortable in the tight quarters, but Layne, a volunteer, views his mission as significant and worth the sacrifice.

"We can come across as just a bunch of yahoos to the general public," Layne says of his fellow enthusiasts. "For years we took pictures of champion pigeons standing in their own crap. That just reinforces the stereotypes. Personally, I like presenting at a higher level." Under Layne's direction, the birds do look rather regal, like the champs they are, and without any droppings beneath them.

The next morning, the last of the Grand Nationals, I witness a most curious spectacle—a Parlor Roller competition. Unlike the other birds at the pageant, Parlor Rollers are prized not so much for their appearance as for their unique abilities. When placed on the ground, Rollers somersault backward like deranged, feathered gymnasts.

No one knows why they do it. They are often grouped with tumblers, a breed that makes backward death spirals in midflight only to recover and continue flying. As with all the other breeds, they must have started with one unusual mutation that was then bred for exaggeration. While the first Parlor Roller may have occasionally spun backward, Rollers today can roll for hundreds of feet.

Although it's hard to see without the benefit of a high-speed camera, a Roller pushes off with its feet and propels itself backward using its wings. Some birds keep their eyes open, while others roll with them closed.

The competition is held several miles away, at a community college soccer field. The fields outside the expo center, although spacious, aren't long enough. Once on site, the reigning champ, Paul Mallard of Bakersfield, California, tells me that one of his birds once rolled 662 feet and one inch. Another rolled 320 feet only to be stopped by a fence. Yet another rolled 448 feet but was stopped by an unfortunately timed sprinkler. "A good bird will roll indefinitely," he says. "It depends on what's in his head. If he has the drive, he won't give up."

The men line up to roll their birds across the soccer field. One man holds a measuring wheel, and one keeps a close eye out for hawks. It's an unusually cold morning, with a bitter wind blowing across the field. Most of us jump up and down in place to stay warm. One at a time, the men cup their birds in one hand and sprint toward the starting line, then bend down and gently start the bird rolling like a bowling ball.

The birds roll quickly, looking like a flurried mass of awkwardly skewed feathers. Why they stop rolling is just as much of a mystery as why they start. But when they finally grind to a halt, they upright themselves, panting. It strikes me that this relentless drive to roll backward is the avian equivalent of an obsessive-compulsive disorder. I ask one of the fanciers why he thinks the birds roll. "Because they're retarded, that's why. If it was a kid, you'd put a helmet on him and stick him in a padded room."

Paul's a bit disappointed with his bird's roll. It stops at 122 feet and 9 inches. "I just don't think he had that many rolls in him today," he confesses. Nonetheless, the high level of competition at the Grand Nationals invigorates Paul. "If I could have a competitive roll like this every week," he says, "I'd be in heaven."

Few animal rights activists share Paul's enthusiasm for the sport. They view the rolling of pigeons as inhumane and actively protest against it. But their disgust with Paul's delight is trivial compared to how they feel about the use of pigeons as live targets at several Pennsylvania gun clubs. *That* sport galvanized thousands of animal rights activists across the nation.

6

Pull!

It's not that we hate pigeons. We treat them well—
until they get shot.

—Robert Tobash, organizer of the
Hegins live pigeon shoot

MY ATTEMPTS TO ENTER THE WORLD OF LIVE PIGEON SHOOTS began with a phone call to the Pike Township Sportsman's Association, one of a handful of clubs in southeastern Pennsylvania where such shoots remain popular. When prompted, the club's president confessed his disdain for pigeons. "They're rats with wings," he said. "Put 'em in your garage and see what a mess they'll make on your car."

But when it came to questions about the pigeon shoots, which his club hosts frequently, he was quicker than an indicted Wall Street CEO to play dumb. "Don't know much about pigeon shooting. It's expensive, that I know. Never done it myself." It didn't take him long, though, to suggest his compatriots a few towns to the west, where Don Bailey, the "pigeon trafficker," lives. "Try the Strausstown club. They shoot a whole lot more than we do."

Given how controversial the sport is and how protective participants are of their hobby, getting into shoots is a challenge. They're held at insular hunting clubs on private property zealously guarded by suspicious members.

But the shooters are breaking no laws: Shooting pigeons for sport is still legal in the state of Pennsylvania. They are, however, skating along the edge of a cultural chasm.

Whether you embrace sport hunting or not, it has earned a legitimate place in our nation's history and cultural landscape. Although it is no longer necessary for survival, many would agree it is a justifiable sport. The animal is stalked, hunted, and eaten. Urbanites tend to snub their noses at hunters, judging them to be bloodthirsty yokels. But to the vast rural population in America, hunting is a way of life, a religion of sorts. It's been passed down from father to son for generations. To proponents, hunting represents an affinity for nature. Most hunters classify themselves as conservationists.

Shooting pigeons for target practice is somehow different. The pigeons aren't stalked and given a chance to outwit the shooter; they're basically slaughtered at close range with shotguns. Why? Well, why not? Pigeons are cheap and plentiful, and targeting them is a lot more fun and challenging than shooting at a clay Frisbee with a predictable arc.

As an American sport, pigeon shoots date back to the 1830s. The sport was imported from England, where the landed gentry enjoyed the expensive challenge of live target practice. The first live pigeon shooting club was born in a suburb of London in 1812. It was named "Old Hats" because the pigeons were released from beneath old bowler hats with a tug of string. The first American pigeon shooting club was formed in Cincinnati about twenty years later.

The early live targets were a mixture of pigeons, blackbirds, purple martins, sparrows, and bats. American trapshooters settled on the docile passenger pigeon as the target of choice because they were so plentiful and easy to capture. At the time, the passenger pigeon was still one of the most prevalent birds in the world.

Pigeon shoots gained enough popularity to support a professional class of marksmen who toured the country with well-attended expositions and vaudeville shows. The life of a professional pigeon shooter was surprisingly lush. Great pigeon shooters were folk heroes who toured the country in lavish railroad cars, dining on the best food and wines as they raked in tens of thousands of dollars in prize money. The shooters were colorful characters dedicated to a life of showmanship. Their rivalries were the stuff of legend, with the general public taking a keen interest in who made it to the top and who was pushed off by a talented newcomer. Such was the rivalry between Doc Carver and Captain Adam H. Bogardus.

Doc Carver, at six-four and 265 pounds a large man for his day, made his name hunting buffalo. By his own estimate, he bagged thirty thousand of the hulking bison, or about sixty buffalo a week for ten years. The Great Plains buffalo was the largest land mammal to roam North America since the Ice Age. In the early 1800s, there were an estimated fifty to sixty million buffalo. By the century's close, there were fewer than a thousand. For his deadly prowess at decimating buffalo, Carver earned the Indian nickname "Evil Spirit of the Plains."

According to some accounts, Doc—who had no medical training—got his nickname from a childhood interest in healing wounded birds and small animals. Born in Illinois in 1840, William Frank Carver left for Minnesota as a teenager to take ownership of his grandfather's land grant. He lived with the Sioux and Pawnee Indians and sharpened his shooting skills. He joined the professional pigeon circuit and beat enough competitors to tour Europe, billing himself as "Champion of the World." He shot for the Prince of Wales, who presented him with a medal, and returned home with a handsome bounty of $80,000 in overall earnings. He was ready to take on the other self-professed Champion of the World—the legendary Captain Bogardus.

Self-promotion aside, Captain Adam H. Bogardus was truly one of the greatest marksmen who ever lived. Born in Albany, New York, Bogardus drifted west to Indiana, where he struggled to make a living as a carpenter. Already known locally for his uncanny sharpshooting, he put down his hammer and picked up his rifle to become a prosperous market hunter. In Chicago, restaurateurs had a strong appetite for his freshly hunted grouse, ducks, turkey, and quail, and he soon became a leading citizen of his town with a reputation for "hitting all that flies."

During the Civil War, Bogardus organized a local militia to fight for the Union and earned the title of captain. A showman at heart, he was rather fond of the appellation and used it prominently for the rest of his life. Bogardus didn't take up pigeon shooting until he was thirty-five, but he was soon traveling the national pigeon circuit to applause and financial reward. Within a year, he had difficulty finding people willing to cough up the money to shoot against him, so he had the following printed in the *Chicago Tribune* in 1869:

> I hereby challenge any man in America to shoot a pigeon match, 50 singles, and 50 double rises for from $500 to

$5,000 a side, according to the rules of the New York Sportsmen's Association. I to use my breech-loading shotgun, my opponent to use any breech-loading gun of any manufacturer he may choose. The match to be shot in Chicago. Man and money ready at my place of business, No. 72 Madison St., Chicago. A. H. Bogardus

To keep busy, Bogardus challenged himself to a variety of crowd-pleasing stunts. He shot birds from a buggy pulled by a horse at full trot. For another stunt, he dropped five hundred birds in 526 minutes using a muzzleloader.

At about this time, animal rights activists and women's organizations teamed up to put an end to the slaughter of innocent birds. Soon enough, many states began passing laws prohibiting the use of pigeons as targets. With politicians putting the kibosh on shooting live pigeons, many shooters turned to alternatives such as glass balls. The balls looked like Christmas ornaments and exploded with a loud pop when hit with birdshot. Fearful that the game might lose some of its romantic luster, many glass-ball manufacturers filled the targets with loose feathers that would simulate a pigeon's feathers sashaying to the ground. Among Bogardus's claims to fame were making the glass ball lighter and inventing a better trap for releasing it.

Bogardus continued his stunts, this time shooting a thousand glass balls in eighty minutes at Manhattan's Madison Square Garden. Later, he would shoot five thousand glass balls in just over six hours with a 97 percent accuracy rate but would lose his hearing in the process. Although hard to relate to in today's world of sports, Bogardus's shooting feats were nothing short of astounding.

For several decades, Bogardus reigned as a titan of the pigeon shooting world. However, Doc Carver issued a challenge in hopes of unseating the champion and winning a life of fame and fortune. Bogardus ducked the challenge for six years before acquiescing to his nemesis in 1883.

The two titans met in Louisville to much public anticipation. Two of the world's finest shooters were finally going to meet, head-to-head, in a live pigeon shoot. Yet even after his arrival, Bogardus continued to duck Carver. On February 21, 1883, the *Louisville Commercial* commented:

> Captain A. H. Bogardus, the champion shot, arrived in the city yesterday morning, and immediately repaired to the Louisville Hotel, where his rival, Dr. Carver, is stopping. Neither of them "recognized" the other, although they met several times during the morning and dined at adjoining tables. Captain Bogardus remarked to a friend in a fatherly way that the "young 'un seemed to be in fine form," and Dr. Carver was overheard saying as he blushed before a plate of potato salad that "the old man was looking pretty well himself." Once or twice they glared politely at each other, and the scene was rather amusing. Captain Bogardus would transfix a baked apple with his fork, and then cast a quick glance at Carver, who at that moment was sipping his oxtail soup, timidly eyeing the Captain over the rim of the bowl.
>
> Thus did the champions dine. Later on they happened to come together at Griffith & Sons establishment (a sporting goods store) and Colonel Joe Griffith stepped

forward and introduced them. The doctor bowed low and acknowledged the presentation, and Bogardus returned the compliment, and for the first time . . . the champions spoke to each other.

The match was held the next day at the Jockey Club. The two marksmen were presented with a hundred live pigeon targets each, released from a series of five traps. It was a close match, the field littered with 165 dead and wounded birds. Doc would squeak past the captain with a score of 83 to 82. He won $500 plus gate money—these matches were attended by thousands—and who knows how much more in side wagers. As with today, gambling was a popular and lucrative aspect of the sport. But more important, Carver had defeated the legendary, and legendarily proud, Captain Bogardus.

Soon thereafter, a sportsman from Cincinnati named George Ligowsky invented the first clay pigeon and concocted a quick, successful way to promote it. He hired the two legends to tour the country and compete in twenty-five tournaments, each in a different city, using his revolutionary targets. The marksmen and audience were pleased, as the new targets were cheaper and less messy, and the lives of tens of thousands of pigeons were spared.

As the tournaments progressed, a demoralized Bogardus would find his shooting rapidly deteriorating. Of the twenty-five matches, a humiliated Bogardus won just three and tied another three. His star fading, he was quoted by newspapers of the time as saying of Carver, "He has beat me."

Bogardus retired from professional shooting at fifty. And what did a retired sharpshooter do in those days? Join the circus, of course. After all, Bogardus was an entertainer who had held large audiences in rapt silence as he performed his miraculous feats. He and four of his sons (he had thirteen children) continued to crisscross the country, first with Buffalo Bill's Wild West vaudeville show and then with other circuses.

Carver also remained true to his showman roots by spending about a year with Buffalo Bill's. He then formed his own traveling show whose dramatic highlight was a horse jumping from a tower into a pool of water. The unusual act became a permanent fixture in Atlantic City until animal rights groups pressured it into closing in the early 1970s.

The last hurrah of live pigeon shoots was at the Paris Olympics of 1900, where it was a gold-medal sport. But a loud outcry from humane societies doomed the sport to just one Olympic showing.

As with Carver and Bogardus, Ligowsky's star would also dim. His invention had a drawback: The all-clay targets had to be tough enough to be catapulted into the air at 60 mph, but they also needed to be delicate enough to blow apart when hit by even just one shotgun pellet, and they often withstood even the full impact of a shotgun blast. His famed clay pigeon would soon be supplanted by a composite made from coal, tar, and pitch. The new shiny black composite pigeons were dubbed Peoria blackbirds.

With the stain of blood expunged from the sport, trapshooting regained its reputation as a wholesome competitive sport. It was respectable enough to attract the active participation of patriotic bandleader John Philip Sousa. He even presided as president of the American Amateur Trapshooting Association from 1916 to 1919.

The last celebrity to lend his name to the sport of live pigeon shooting was the king of machismo himself, Ernest Hemingway, who targeted pigeons legally—and with glee—when he lived in Cuba. "The same people who crusade against fighting cocks also blast you for the pigeon shoot," Hemingway told his friend and chronicler A. E. Hotchner. "Although it's barred in a lot of places it's legal here and it's the most exciting betting-sport I know . . ."

Hemingway developed an appetite for rock doves earlier in his career. When living as a poor writer in Paris, he had found them to be a unique and inexpensive source of protein for his young family. "[I] am also fond of the Jardin [du Luxembourg]," Hemingway wrote to Hotchner, "because it kept us from starvation . . . On days when the dinner pot was absolutely devoid of content, I would put Mr. Bumby . . . into the baby carriage and wheel him over to the Jardin. Once my selection was made, it was a simple matter to entice my victim with the corn, snatch him, wring his neck, and flip his carcass under Mr. Bumby's blanket."

While Hemingway could make just about anything brutish sound romantic, even an outlaw sport, modern-day pigeon shoots have little of the cachet they possessed in the heyday of Doc Carver and Captain Bogardus. Today's shooters live in a murky underground of unpublicized competitions and frequent lawsuits.

Don Bailey lives in a highly trafficked area. That is to say, he sleeps, eats, and watches television about seventy-five feet from Interstate 78, where tens of thousands of cars and trucks barrel past his backyard daily. Unlike wealthier neighborhoods that lobby for costly noise barriers, Bailey's meets the interstate at about grade. The only thing separating his family's trailer-like ranch house from the speeding westbound traffic is a metal guardrail and a simple chain-link fence.

You can spot his pigeon coops as you head onto the off-ramp and jog around the interchange to his house, about two blocks away. I expect to be greeted by grizzled old Bailey, and I'm surprised when an attractive young woman named Jenna answers the door. Her grandfather, she tells me, has just left to attend a shoot about an hour away and will play cards afterward. He won't be back until midnight, and he'll be leaving the house before dawn to set up for the pigeon shoot down the road in Strausstown.

Jenna is kind enough to invite me in for a glass of water and show me around the backyard. Against the persistent roar of speeding trucks, she guides me to the pigeon coops, just feet away from the interstate. Inside, a wide variety of pigeon breeds peck around the concrete and wait. Many of the pigeons are the scruffy ones you see on city streets, probably because they *were* on city streets just days before their poaching.

I am dismayed to recognize several show and racing birds. Without a doubt, there are several homers that were kicked off the team and sold to the lowest bidder— the pigeon brokers. I also see several fancy pigeons with distinctive colorings and physiologies.

"Where does he get them?" I ask.

"People bring them to him. Lots of people."

Live pigeon shoots popped onto the cultural landscape in the late 1980s, when animal rights activists targeted one particularly gruesome public competition in southeastern Pennsylvania—the annual Hegins Labor Day pigeon shoot. Some communities hold bake sales and barbecues to raise funds, others tag sales and craft fairs. Hegins slaughtered pigeons. Since 1933, the small hamlet of Hegins (pop. 850) has held a pigeon shoot at the town park to raise money for ball fields, playground equipment, and other civic improvements.

The pigeon shoots never attracted much attention; Hegins is just another Appalachian coal mining town with no real claim to fame. Most years the shoot consisted of a hundred marksmen and a few hundred local families picnicking to the staccato bursts of gunfire and falling pigeons. The shoot usually raised about $5,000.

But once animal rights activists learned of the annual competition, Hegins became their rallying cry, and thousands descended on the community from all across the country. In short order, Hegins's unusual tradition was thrust into the national spotlight, and the town became the epicenter of a culture war. Activists accused residents of brutality and gave the town a media-friendly moniker: "Cruelty Capital of the World." Locals viewed the protesters as urban elitists assaulting the town's traditional values as well as their right to bear arms.

Year after year, the event took on a macabre carnival atmosphere. Attendance actually increased as people across the region came to watch spectators and activists clash. So many people flooded the shoot that the village started charging admission. Even the local KKK came to show its support for the event. Some spectators wore T-shirts emblazoned with slogans like "Hegins Labor Day Shoot—Where Flags and Feathers Fly!"

Things soon got a little out of hand, with some in the audience performing unpleasant stunts reminiscent of

Ozzy Osborne's salad days, like biting the head off a wounded bird and dancing a taunting jig. Others played Hacky Sack with the birds or stuck them on forks and lit them on fire.

A live pigeon shoot works like this: Pigeons from all over the region are trapped and then sold to a broker like Don Bailey. The birds are kept in crowded cages with marginal food and water until the broker sells them to the event organizers. Since at this point they're basically commodities, much like pork bellies, the price paid per pigeon fluctuates, often between three and six dollars a bird.

Marksmen interested in participating pay a fee of about $150, which gives them the chance to take aim at roughly twenty to twenty-five birds. The killing grounds are shaped like a fenced-in lopsided circle with an approximate diameter of fifty feet. The circle's center is lined with about half a dozen traps, which are electronically opened by a trap operator. Each trap is hastily stuffed with a crouching pigeon. The marksman doesn't know which trap the operator will randomly choose to open, further adding to the challenge.

The marksman stands just outside the circle, about twenty-five yards from the traps, and takes aim with a double-barreled shotgun. To score a point, the marksman must hit the bird, and the bird must fall within the prescribed circle. If the bird is blasted full of birdshot but falls outside the fenced-in circle to die, the shot doesn't count and no point is scored.

The pigeons are kept in makeshift huts behind the shooter. Here they await their fate to the repetitive drumbeat of shotgun blasts. For the pigeons, it's a bit like the Russian roulette scene in *The Deer Hunter*. They don't know when they will be chosen to play, and once they are "playing," they don't know if luck will earn them an empty chamber or, in this case, a badly targeted shot.

After each shot, a trapper boy refills the empty trap with another pigeon, and the marksman reloads. Another randomly chosen trap is sprung open, and the marksman aims for feathers. If there were twenty-five tries in a round, then a perfect score would be twenty-five birds lying inside the circle in varying states of consciousness. Someone who can shoot a perfect score is, well, a rare bird.

After a round is finished, the trapper boys, ranging in age from eight to eighteen, scoop up the dead and wounded birds and bring them back to the shed. Along the way, they usually snap the birds' necks by giving them a twirl or banging them against a hard object. At the Hegins holiday shoot, the trapper boys often hammed it up by crushing the birds with their bodies and tearing off the birds' heads for the spectators' enjoyment. Still, many of the wounded birds made it back to the shed alive, where they were squeezed into large plastic garbage bags filled with other dead and dying birds, and left to suffocate.

More than five thousand pigeons were sacrificed each year at the Hegins shoot in the name of civic fundraising and perhaps even community service—they were eradicating vermin, were they not? Of those, only about 25 percent of the birds were killed instantly. A lucky few flew away unharmed. The vast majority lay in the grass, suffering an agonizingly slow death.

In the old days, the pigeons were at least gathered up and eaten. Pigeon potpie was once a popular post-shoot delicacy in Hegins. These days pigeons are regarded as suspect, perhaps poisoned or carrying disease. Consequently, they are burned in big trash barrels or sent to a rendering facility after the shoot is over.

That accounts for only some of the birds—the ones shot so quickly that they barely made it off the ground, let alone out of the circle. Then there are the birds that make it a little farther into the air before being blasted full of buckshot. These pigeons inevitably fall back to earth, either tumbling slowly through the air with wings askew or crashing like lead weights. Once on the ground, they often stumble around with broken wings and missing body parts before coming to rest and waiting to die of their wounds or starvation. Then there are the birds that are hit with some birdshot, though not enough to bring them down. They fly into the woods to die a slower death.

At Hegins, the activists were forbidden to enter the circle area, and they were not allowed to collect the badly wounded pigeons until well after the shoot was over. By that time, the gasping birds had spent the better part of a day twitching on the ground, much like a soldier whose comrades are unable to retrieve him during a heavy and prolonged firefight.

The injured pigeons that flew back toward the park were more easily retrievable. It was these birds that the protesters had to race to retrieve before a spectator, also running at full speed, killed it for fun and showmanship. When an animal rights activist did retrieve a bird in time, it was brought to an animal ambulance, where a volunteer veterinarian decided whether it could be saved or would be humanely euthanized.

At the end of the shoot, activists bought any surplus birds. Organizers knew they had the activists over a barrel and charged exorbitant sums. The protesters could at least take comfort in knowing that the pigeons would spend the rest of their lives in an avian sanctuary.

After thirteen years of aggressive protests and countless lawsuits, the activists' siege took its toll on Hegins. A unanimous ruling from the Pennsylvania Supreme Court tipped the balance, permitting employees of the Pennsylvania Society for the Prevention of Cruelty to Animals to cite shooters for animal brutality. Hegins would have to open its gates to the enemy—in this case, an animal protection officer from Philadelphia.

Organizers of the event weren't about to let a city bureaucrat cite their paying guests for animal abuse. After sixty-five years of concentrated slaughter and fun, they killed the shoot. The pigeons had won the day. "We are not willing to subject our townspeople to additional violence and terrorism by a group of out-of-state individuals who feel they are morally superior to our citizens," responded Robert Tobash, a local insurance salesman and leader of the Hegins Labor Day Committee. "We will not give one person from Philadelphia the opportunity to enforce his private version of the Pennsylvania animal cruelty laws, which, for the past hundred years, have been interpreted to allow the shooting of pigeons."

Rather than replace the pigeons with skeet, or hold a craft fair or volleyball tournament, Hegins closed up shop altogether. Nowadays Labor Day at the park is a decidedly subdued affair. The town rents the small open-air pavilions for family cookouts and reunions.

Pigeon shoots remain legal in Pennsylvania, at least for now. The ruling merely addressed a procedural issue stemming from a lower court. Meanwhile, pigeon shoots continue weekly at private hunt clubs, such as the Strausstown Rod and Gun Club. As well as filing legal challenges to the sport, activists have lobbied the state legislature hard for over a decade to outlaw the shoots, but proposed bills either never make it to the floor or lack enough votes. Harrisburg is a conservative town located right in the middle of hunt country.

While pigeon shoots are held below the radar in several other states, southeastern Pennsylvania remains a hot spot for gunning down large quantities of feral pigeons for target practice. There's little doubt, though, that the sportsmen of southeastern Pennsylvania are feeling squeezed. Self-professed conservationists, they watch in simmering resignation as their families' treasured hunting grounds are swallowed up by suburban sprawl. It's now nearly impossible to hunt with a rifle without hitting a residential neighborhood. And after generations of working the soil and mining what's beneath it, their children are forced to seek economic opportunities in the wildlife barren and culturally antagonistic cities.

Hunting itself is dwindling as a sport. Even the animal rights groups, who continue to keep an eye on the private gun clubs, say the number of participants in the pigeon shoots is declining. According to the U.S. Fish and Wildlife Service, the number of hunters declined 22 percent to 13 million between 1985 and 2001. Pennsylvania alone lost fifty thousand hunters between 1991 and 2001. With urban population trends on their side, animal rights activists openly boast that the total demise of hunting is "just a generation away!"

★ ★ ★

"Dr. Pigeon sent me," I say to the fat man in the jalopy. "He said you would talk to me."

It's a frigid predawn morning, and I'm once again standing outside the house of Don Bailey, the man animal rights activists love to hate and pigeon shooters depend on. I knew he wouldn't be a big talker. He is, however, my ticket into the Strausstown Rod and Gun Club. Which is why I find myself at the edge of the driveway pleading my case and shamelessly dropping the name of Dr. Pigeon. Bailey is a large-framed man with disheveled gray hair and a stubbly beard. This morning he tells me that he's heading out to pick up "his Mexican boys" who help him set up the shoot.

Perhaps I could help him set up, I suggest. "You've got to be a member," he says. "It's members only—only members can step on the property . . . We wouldn't want anybody to get hurt."

Did he mean me? Given the avalanche of bad publicity and countless lawsuits they've suffered through, I knew club members would be wary of strangers showing an interest in their controversial hobby.

"But Dr. Pigeon sent me," I say meekly. "He said you'd help me out." Bailey pauses. He and the good doctor are friendly acquaintances. His truck stalls. An anemic sun begins to emerge from the foothills beyond. I try out one more line: "Maybe I could shoot some pigeons, too?"

After a long pause, Bailey says, "Meet me at the club at around eleven. Park across the street."

"Should I walk over to the club to announce my arrival?"

"We'll know you're there."

Bailey is right, of course. It doesn't take long for club members to spot my hunter-green Subaru parked across the road. Dressed in old jeans, clodhopper boots, a canvas work jacket, and a new baseball cap, I'm hoping against hope that I might pass for a local. Moments later, a pickup truck drives up and blocks my car. A well-dressed man is behind the wheel. Two burly men get out and fold their arms across their chests.

"Are you here representing some kind of animal rights organization?" the driver asks.

"No. I'm writing a book."

"Well I got two witnesses recording your answer . . . What's this book about?"

Before I can answer, one of the burly men eyes my license plates. No matter how I tried to angle the car, there was just no hiding my Achilles' heel. "You from Massachusetts?" he asks with obvious disgust. "You some kind of friend of Ted Kennedy?"

"I was hoping I might get a chance to shoot some birds myself. Would that be possible?"

The man driving the truck, who introduces himself as Kee Bubbenmoyer, invites me into the club, a low-slung building with a big dark-paneled central room crowded by tables. The lights are turned low, but I can make out a long bar with a country-music jukebox at one end of the room and a short-order counter for hot dogs and hamburgers across the way. Bubbenmoyer buys me a cup of coffee and motions for me to join him at one of the better-lit tables beside a window. Outside, shotgun after shotgun blasts away, littering the ground with pigeons.

While I remain conflicted about hunting—at least hunters are honest about where meat comes from—I find shooting any animal for target practice repellent. As a kid, I shot a robin with a BB gun. It felt like an accomplishment until I walked up and saw the bird twitching on the ground. It took three more rounds to put it out of its misery, and that kind of soured me on shooting animals. But if the price of entry to the gun club is shooting at a pigeon, then so be it. I'm a crappy shot, anyway.

Bubbenmoyer is a well-spoken middle-aged man with a slight paunch and inquisitive eyes. While his demeanor is friendly, he eyes me suspiciously the entire time. As chairman of the Lehigh Valley Friends of the NRA and a charter member of the Pennsylvania Flyers Association, a local group devoted to protecting pigeon shooting, Bubbenmoyer is considered a good spokesman for the sport.

"A pigeon in this state is not protected under the game laws," he says. "There is no provision that deals with pigeons. There's no pigeon season and no bag limit. Shooting pigeons is our legal right, and nobody is going to take it away from us."

We are interrupted several times by other club members walking up to our table to place orders with Bubbenmoyer for deer cuts and sausages. "How much product do you want?" Bubbenmoyer asks, referring to the freshly hunted deer carcasses. Apparently, he takes orders for a butcher.

I ask him why pigeons in particular are targeted. "Pigeons fly best in this situation, and they're readily available—they're a by-product of our society. Blue jays are protected under the migratory bird laws, and starlings aren't available. Where are you going to catch starlings?"

According to Bubbenmoyer, pigeons used for the shoots are gathered by local farm kids, often Amish and

Mennonite, and sold to Don Bailey for a buck or two apiece. Sometimes professionals use cannon nets to catch hundreds at a time in a field or a city park. Show birds and homers are also culled from their flocks.

"If we didn't provide a market for culled birds, their necks would be wrung and they'd be thrown out anyway," Bubbenmoyer says. "If you can believe it, [the activists] want us to euthanize all our birds at a vet's office with a lethal injection. Can you imagine how everybody—let alone poultry farmers—would be affected by such a stupid law?"

The club charges about $5 a pigeon. A twenty-five-bird match costs roughly $125. By comparison, a clay pigeon costs about five cents. Although most marksmen would deny it, there is still money to be made in the sport through friendly wagering that can run into the thousands.

"It's an expensive sport," Bubbenmoyer allows. "But I wouldn't use the word 'elite.' You got everybody here, from guys in construction to doctors and lawyers." A quick survey of the lot outside the window proves his point. Ratty old pickups like Bailey's are parked beside new BMWs and Mercedeses.

Pigeon shooting is alive and well, according to Bubbenmoyer. "On any given day, there's at least one shoot going on in this state. Shooting's very popular in these parts . . . Actually, pigeon shoots are popular all over. Just this year I shot in ten states, and I couldn't make every shoot I was invited to." Bubbenmoyer wouldn't name the states for fear that they, too, would be embroiled in activist lawsuits. "They want us out of business, period."

Bubbenmoyer cultivated his love of targeting pigeons four decades ago, as a young boy. "We used to go to the sweet-corn farms where the pigeons would feed in the fields. We'd shoot 'em as sport, and we'd eat 'em. It was a lot of fun. Hell, back then every bar in these coal-mining towns had a Saturday pigeon shoot in their back-yard. After a shoot, there'd be families lined up to take pigeons home to eat. Whatever was left was hauled away to orphanages . . . Personally, I always liked my birds baked with onions and celery, or grilled. Breasting them was easy. They'd come right off."

Bubbenmoyer paints a rosy and sentimental picture of pigeon shooting. He also likes to expound on several basic National Rifle Association talking points: "Sport hunting is what pays for all the wildlife in this country; without hunters and fishermen, there wouldn't be any wild-life." The basis of his argument is that if wildlife ceased to have an economic benefit, it would cease to exist, because hunters protect—or "conserve"—what they hunt.

He's partly right. Hunters do pay a lot of money for state fees and permits, and that money goes straight to conservation programs. There is also a federal gun tax. That revenue also goes to federal conservation programs, which manage wildlife so it can regenerate and be hunted for years to come.

To Bubbenmoyer, the battle with animal rights ac-tivists is about more than shooting pigeons. It's about who controls the future of outdoor recreation. "The *animalists* want to let nature take care of itself, and they want us all to be vegetarians . . . Their problem is that they subscribe to anthropomorphism. They think animals are people. Well, they're not. Animals have a different set of nervous systems. They feel pain differently. They don't possess this," he says, pointing to his brain. "I've seen pigeons, all shot up, get up and start pecking around for food.

Now, if I broke your arm, would you be craving a lobster tail?"

The way he views animals is a result of his rural upbringing. "I grew up with an agricultural background. One of my grandfathers had a farm, and the other one ran a slaughterhouse. I understand that animals die. And I still cry when my dog dies. But animals are still different."

He claims the "animalists" are historical revisionists who rewrite history to suit their cause and blacken the good name of hunters. According to Bubbenmoyer, hunters didn't exterminate the buffalo—the government did it to control the Indians—and passenger pigeons weren't overhunted; they succumbed to disease and a changing habitat.

As Bubbenmoyer tells it, the gun club is basically performing a community service, much like volunteering to adopt a highway. They're ridding the area of disease-carrying vermin that would otherwise be costly to address. "Hell, when it comes to protecting a bridge or a building, it can cost eighty thousand dollars just for the netting," he explains.

The activists are on some sort of deranged crusade, according to Bubbenmoyer. He is at least partly correct— most animal rights activists ultimately want to take away these people's right to hunt. "Yeah, I'm bitter about it," Bubbenmoyer says, his anger escalating. "They told us we are living our life wrong. Sure, they don't shoot pigeons in Center City, Philadelphia, but they got a lot of other problems . . . In my culture, we don't need keys, we don't lock our doors, and we don't have crack houses and murders down the street, either . . . Frankly, I like my way of life more than theirs, but I'm not protesting what they're doing. And yet they want to impose their values on us. I can't even relate to how they think."

Just as the activists had to absorb slews of insults at Hegins, Bubbenmoyer says he and his friends have had to put up with an avalanche of abuse as well. "We were just supposed to take their vile comments and diatribes about us butt-fucking our kids and each other like deranged hill-billies. It was pure filth, and they said it right in front of our kids. We stood and took it for weeks. They were lucky that we didn't come down there and take them on. Those people portray themselves as kind and caring, but they're fanatics that will go to any extreme."

A friend interrupts to inform Bubbenmoyer that it's his turn to shoot. Bubbenmoyer cuts short his tirade and invites me to watch and then participate. We cross the parking lot in the bitter cold and head to the shooting range. There are three rings set up so three marksmen can compete simultaneously.

Bubbenmoyer walks up to the circle with his double-barrel twelve-gauge shotgun. In front of him are fields lit-tered with spent shells, feathers, and dead pigeons. To his side, in a small shed, is the trap operator, who presses a button to pull open a trap whenever a shooter shouts, "Pull!" Today the trap operator has something special that he wants to share with Bubbenmoyer. He pulls a bloody deer head out of a plastic trash bag and holds it up for all to see. "Got this with a muzzleloader! Pretty nice, huh?"

Bubbenmoyer eyes the range and braces the shot-gun against his shoulder. He yells, "Pull!" A gray and white pigeon scrambles out of a spring-loaded trap. It looks around and furiously pumps its wings until it is about eight feet off the ground. But before it can settle on a direction, Bubbenmoyer blasts it out of the air with a well-aimed trajectory of lead pellets. Feathers fly everywhere and gently float to the ground. Pumped full of lead, the bird can't even hover. It just smashes right into the ground.

Bubbenmoyer hits two more. One is a few feet off the ground. Another is about fifteen feet up and headed toward the safety of trees before it tumbles awkwardly back to earth. The bird tries repeatedly to get up to walk, but with two broken wings, it finds balancing difficult and keeps falling down. Another lies on its side, fluttering one wing. The fourth gets away, and a fifth is partially hit and continues flying into the woods.

After Bubbenmoyer finishes, the trapper boys run into the circle to collect the dead and injured birds. They look about fourteen years old and tell me they will be paid $50 for their labor. They pick up the birds off the frozen ground and run them back to a small lean-to where they stuff them into clear plastic garbage bags filled with other bloodied birds weakly trying to move about and get air. The trapper boys tell me, "Bailey takes them wherever he takes them. We just throw them on the back of his truck." Because of his health, Bailey doesn't participate in the shoots. He sits comfortably in his truck nearby and keeps a close eye on the action.

Alongside the bags of birds in the lean-to are cages filled with more targets. A few birds have somehow escaped, and I see them pecking for food around the lean-to. I feel like pleading with them to fly away from here, but they just walk around contentedly, oblivious to the carnage all around them. Perhaps Bubbenmoyer *is* right. Maybe they are inherently stupid creatures. Or are they just disoriented?

Bubbenmoyer points his gun toward the ground and walks away from the shooting circle. "The animalists say it's like shooting fish in a barrel," he tells me. "But that's just the rhetoric of the other side. As you can see, it's the toughest shot game there is. To give you an idea, the last time a guy hit twenty-five straight was three years ago, and he was a top gun."

Now it's my turn. Bubbenmoyer hands me his shotgun. "Ever shot one of these before?" he asks.

"Once," I say nervously.

"Well, there's a lot of kickback, so why don't you practice firing it first so you know what it's like." He shows me how to load the gun and snap it back shut. I aim for the steep bank at the end of the range. The gun jumps back against my shoulder, but I hold my stance so as not to further embarrass myself. The air smells of sulfur. My fingers are numb from the cold steel. But all things considered, I enjoy the rush. I don't know what it is, but there's something gratifying about firing a gun.

"Not bad," Bubbenmoyer says in a calm, paternal voice. "I think you're ready. What do you think?"

"Sure," I say hesitantly. "Let's give it a go."

I step back up to the shooting line, load the gun with two red shotgun shells, and snap the gun shut. There is no safety to release. Bubbenmoyer stands back ten feet with a cluster of other men. They eye me carefully. This is the litmus test. Am I full of shit—an animalist in disguise—or a regular guy who is going to give them a fair shake in my book?

"Pull!" I grunt, surprised at the ease with which the word passes my lips.

A blue and gray pigeon catapults out of the trap. Unlike a practiced shooter, I am unable to aim quickly, and the bird gains twenty feet and swerves to the left before my brain instructs my finger to pull the trigger. I completely miss the target. It would be convenient to say that I purposely miss the target. But somehow this isn't the case. Frankly, I am surprised and disappointed by my aim. How hard can this be? I'm firing two shotgun shells brimming with lead pellets, and yet I didn't even come close to hitting the bird.

"Pull!"

I manage to target the next pigeon just ten feet off the ground, but once again, I miss. While I take some comfort in how my lousy aim has spared the life of the pigeon, I am conflicted. The competitive edge takes over. I *want* to hit one of the damn things. I want to feel that sense of elation akin to sinking a pool ball into a corner pocket.

"Pull!"

Another pigeon heads for the trees, uninjured. The satisfaction I feel firing the shotgun is now overshadowed by something else I hadn't predicted: I want to impress Bubbenmoyer and his friends. If not impress, then at least not humiliate myself. I am stunned by how difficult hitting a bird with a blanket of lead can be.

"Pull!"

Not even a feather.

"Pull!"

I have a split second to line up the pigeon in my sights and make a best guess at where the bird is headed. An explosion, a cloud of smoke, and a modest puff of feathers. I hit some part of the bird's anatomy, but just barely. The pigeon, barely breaking stride, flees to the safety of the forest. A handful of feathers drifts to the ground. My injured pride is momentarily rescued by a pigeon with one or two lead pellets painfully embedded in its flesh.

I leave the shooting line frustrated. If only I could have another round, I'm sure I can bag a bird. I say my goodbyes. On my way back to my car, I pass several pigeons that have crashed haphazardly into the parking lot. Their heads are twisted, their wings and legs skewed in unnatural poses. Blood pools beside their beaks and stains the gravel. By day's end, more than a thousand birds will be targeted in the name of sport and tradition.

I jump into my car, feeling sickened and ashamed. I drive down the dirt road, past the pine trees that hide the spectacle from prying eyes, past the three dozen "no trespassing" signs to make parking by meddlesome activists impossible, and past Don Bailey's house. I pull onto the interstate and head east toward home.

I had journeyed to the cultural depths of pigeon hating. I partook in a sport that repulses just about everyone I know, including pigeon people, and now I feel like I need a shower. I long for a swing on the pendulum back to "normal" pigeon folks, those obsessed with living pigeons, enough to live with them in birdhouses. My spring travels will give me just that opportunity, in spades. And yet the hatred is never far away.

Spring

7

Inside the Cuckoo Clock

ORLANDO MARTINEZ OPENS THE DOOR TO HIS BEDROOM closet and starts climbing up a makeshift ladder mounted against the wall. Seconds later, he pokes his head up through a trapdoor in the ceiling into a homemade crawl space. He is quickly surrounded by dozens of softly cooing pigeons basking in the filtered sunlight of a brisk spring morning. Above him is another trapdoor with a Plexiglas cover that leads to the roof.

Orlando takes a deep breath and surveys his young birds, pigeons born mere months ago. The product of generations of careful breeding, these baby birds will shoulder Orlando's ambition to win the Main Event in six months. They may be mere tikes now, but within weeks they will begin intensive physical training that will transform them into Olympian athletes capable of flying hundreds of miles at incredible speeds.

The smell inside the coop is organic—a dusty mixture of corn, seeds, and droppings. The pigeons calmly groom one another and peck at leftover feed as Orlando moves about, gently scooping up a pigeon here and there to routinely inspect its wings and carriage. "Just being around them makes me happy," he says.

While most potential buyers inspect a home's infrastructure and fret about its location before buying it, Orlando's concerns lay elsewhere. "The first thing I checked out was the view on the roof. It was good for racing. It's the reason I bought this house—to raise pigeons."

Orlando and his pigeons live under the same roof, with the loft above resembling an oversized cuckoo clock. One of the first modifications Orlando made to his house was to carve big holes in the roof and ceiling so his pigeons could sleep in a crawl space above his bedroom closet. He even built the pigeons a miniature staircase so they could move back and forth more easily between their cozy indoor perches and their sunny wire mesh home outside.

Little if any of Orlando's enthusiasm is visible in his own living quarters: a large ramshackle space with one table, four chairs, a neglected stereo in one corner, an old fridge in another, and a half-finished sleeping loft. But Orlando has big plans for the coop that houses his young birds. "I'm getting them an air filtering system, so their air is better than what I breathe downstairs," he says. "I'm putting in a water purification system, even though I drink city water. And I hope to put in a central vacuum system for them, which is going to really piss off Omayra, because we don't even have one. Now do you understand the mentality of a pigeon racer? Oh yeah, the floor's heated, too."

As Orlando relaxes in the coop, chaos is breaking out down below. Topí, his rambunctious pit bull with a fondness for salted codfish, enters the bedroom closet and steals several pieces of Omayra's laundry, then turns his attention to Orlando's two parrots, Coco and Isabelle. With a pair of panties tightly clenched in his mouth, the dog chases the parrots around the house. The phone is ringing, and

Orlando's mother shouts for him from downstairs. Omayra chases Topí, trying to get her panties back. The parrots find a safe perch and begin their favorite eardrum-piercing imitation—an impossibly shrill ringing cell phone.

Orlando sighs and climbs down from the coop. He ignores the noise and heads for the backyard, where his old birds—any bird born in the prior year and before—live in a second, larger coop. To the uninitiated, a big coop can be a mildly frightening place filled with fluttering wings, more reminiscent of Alfred Hitchcock's *The Birds* than Edward Hicks's *Peaceable Kingdom*. But upon closer inspection, the old birds are rather sedate, even as Orlando walks around and picks them up. And they are, without a doubt, a handsome lot. Their postures are erect, their breasts muscular, and their gray and white feathers long and elegant. Most strikingly, they're clean.

Orlando picks up #231 and stares into her piercing red eyes. When each bird is born, a small aluminum band indicating the bird's number and racing club is placed around its ankle. Unlike a racing band, it cannot be removed. Because fanciers have so many birds—Orlando has 120—they rarely name them, usually referring to the anklet number instead.

"This bird won at least three races, big ones," Orlando says of #231. "She's the type of pigeon who told me she'd win because of her appearance. Her children are the same way. They all give me that same look, that same appearance. I can't explain it. It's almost like she's looking at me and talking to me. Both her daughters are winners, and now the granddaughter is, too."

Orlando, with Omayra's help, spends countless hours feeding his homers, cleaning them, vaccinating them, monitoring them, and making repairs to his coops. It's not a cheap hobby. To Omayra's chagrin, Orlando spends about $4,000 a year on enough antibiotics, vitamins, supplements, and vaccinations to transform his clothes closets into aviary medicine cabinets.

"Some guys think they can just spray some water around and dust the coop with some feed," Orlando says with a look of disgust. "There's so much to it that I couldn't possibly explain it all. I'd need a month."

Pomposity aside, I suspect Orlando is telling me the truth. He does have an encyclopedic knowledge of his pigeons, stemming from a near-lifetime of devotion. Orlando couldn't stop thinking about his birds even if he wanted to. He's practically a slave to his hobby. But his affliction is mild, to say the least, when compared to that of Dave Roth—Arizona's very own Don Quixote—who lives in a birdhouse.

Maricopa County, Arizona, prides itself on being tough on crime. The county's sheriff, Joe Arpaio, is the self-proclaimed "toughest sheriff in America." Upon taking office in 1993, Arpaio took on the county prisons just outside Phoenix. "Jails should not be country clubs," he declared. In short order, inmates from overcrowded jails were housed in tent cities, hot lunches were replaced with baloney sandwiches, and prisoners were made to work in chain gangs and even wear pink underwear.

The Maricopa County jail, where suspects await trial in downtown Phoenix, precedes Arpaio by nearly a decade, and its facilities leave much to be desired. The ten-story structure takes up an entire city block. It looks particularly imposing because there are no windows to break up its concrete and brick facade. Instead, the jail has layers of giant louvers that help ventilate the building and give it the appearance of a power station.

While few prisoners might recommend its living arrangements, pigeons were once proud to call it home by the thousands. They roosted on the ledges, on the giant awning over the entrance, and particularly favored the horizontal vents stretching across the building like masonry scars. It was perfect territory for feral rock doves, full of ridges and near a perpetual food source: scraps of food left behind by downtown pedestrians. So they did what pigeons do when they make a happy home—they multiplied and shat all over the place.

The sidewalk was full of it, as were the steps leading to the entrance, and, of course, the entrance awning. Something had to be done. It was a government building run by a spit-and-polish paramilitary organization. Even mighty Joe Arpaio had been shat on. A "tough on pigeons" policy was quickly formulated. The county would place poisoned perches on the ledges. The poison would be absorbed into the birds' bloodstream through their feet. End of story . . . Well, not quite.

A few miles away, on the outskirts of downtown Phoenix, a man named Dave Roth lived in a modest ranch house where he regularly scanned the news for anything to do with pigeons. A lonely bachelor then in his early forties, Roth had dropped out of conventional life and dedicated his life to crusading for pigeons. His sworn enemies at the time were the pest control companies that poisoned pigeons, and the "imbeciles" who agreed to hire them.

As a former public relations officer for the local fire department, Roth knew how to get a reporter's ear. Within days, the newspapers and television stations were all carrying the story, but with one difference—they were using information that Roth had passed on to them. Rather than pitting the county against a few bunny huggers, the news stories now contained well-researched information about the hazards of poisons, alternative options, and a cost-benefit analysis of the various methods.

A simple plan to rid a downtown jail of pigeon poop had turned into a complicated debate on avian population control. Roth couldn't have been happier. As the founder of the Urban Wildlife Society, he declared that his mission was to educate. Roth spent the following days ramping up his aggressive press campaign. He organized a demonstration outside the jail, replete with photogenic children carrying picket signs. He made his rounds to all the press organizations with his favorite pigeon, Tootsie, proudly perched on his shoulder. Tootsie shat on a number of desks and articles of newsroom clothing, but she also charmed the pants off columnists, editorial writers, and reporters alike. Roth even took Tootsie to meetings of the county board of supervisors, where she similarly cleared her bowels and worked her charms.

With Tootsie in tow, Roth may have looked like a pirate, or even a loon, but his arguments were sound. The use of poison had many drawbacks: The birds could suffer for up to thirty-six hours and often in front of horrified pedestrians; children could come into contact with the poison; raptors (such as Phoenix's protected peregrine falcons) might eat a poisoned pigeon; and, perhaps most important, poisons solved the problem only temporarily. Poison might make the problem go away but, as they say, nature abhors a vacuum, and new residents quickly replaced those violently evicted.

Destroying pigeon populations is like continuously bailing out a rowboat instead of plugging up the hole. It's high-maintenance and ineffective. Roth even produced a letter from the National Pest Management Association that supported his cause:

> While the strategy of bird removal (trapping and/or lethal baiting) reduces the population, it only offers a temporary solution to the problem. Birds will migrate back into the area and re-inhabit previous roosting sites if they are not excluded from the site. So in either case, for long-term bird management, exclusion is essential.

While others were arguing about the inhumanity of poison—catch-and-release became another popular alternative—Roth focused the debate on something more tangible to the politicians and taxpayers: money. He advocated netting the prison louvers and stringing a low-voltage wire along the ledges. The up-front investment appeared steep compared to other methods: $30,000 versus just $10,000 for the poison. But the poison would have to be reapplied yearly and would still involve cleaning up pigeon poop, while netting and wiring were a permanent solution. As it was, the county was already spending $20,000 a year to clean up after the birds outside the jail. Roth argued that the more humane method would result in a savings of $1 million over the course of the next few decades. Take away the pigeons' ability to roost, and the problem would be gone for good.

"We were lucky to get Dave involved," says County Supervisor Mary Rose Wilcox, whose district spans most of downtown, when I call her. "Bureaucracies usually take the easiest route. Killing looked like the easiest thing to do. But then Dave stepped in and gave us a better alternative. A lot of people thought he was kooky for caring about pigeons, but I thought he was pretty cool."

I first discovered Roth while browsing the Internet for stories related to bird control. His Web site, Urban Wildlife Society, kept popping up on my Google searches —a fact Roth is delighted by, given that he spends endless hours each week updating it all by his lonesome. The Urban Wildlife Society, I would soon learn, was a society of one obsessed workaholic.

Situated in the Sonora Desert with summer temperatures routinely in the triple digits, Phoenix didn't strike me as a particularly hospitable place to live, let alone visit. Although the city was settled in 1870, its population didn't start rising dramatically until the invention of air-conditioning and a diversion of the Colorado River's water. It is now one of the fastest-growing cities in America. Freeways and housing complexes reminiscent of Los Angeles are bursting from the desert like popcorn.

Pigeons, it would seem, have also taken a liking to Phoenix. They're everywhere, from suburban strip malls to downtown parking garages and sidewalks. Given that pigeons aren't indigenous to this continent, let alone the American Southwest, one can safely surmise that they were brought here as racers, breeders, and pets and are either escapees or were purposely let loose. It's a testament to their adaptability that this migrationless species can survive the heat of an Arizona summer.

Dave Roth lives just north of town in a modest neighborhood of ranch houses and tidy lawns that wouldn't look out of place as a *Brady Bunch* backdrop—that is, except Roth's own dilapidated abode. A van and a compact car sit in the cracked asphalt driveway, badly in need of cosmetic attention and speckled in pigeon droppings. The van, which bears a resemblance to the groovy Scooby-Doo Mystery Machine, slumps unevenly on two flat tires.

Roth meets me just outside what functions as his front door. "Welcome!" he bellows enthusiastically. "Welcome to international headquarters." Roth is dressed in elastic black gym shorts, a black T-shirt (a Bob Seger concert souvenir circa 1996), and imitation Birkenstock sandals. With his mane of wavy black hair, graying beard, expanding waist, and aviator sunglasses, he looks an awful lot like a nebbish Jerry Garcia.

When I ask to see the inside of his home, Roth looks concerned. Hesitantly, he invites me inside. We enter through the front door, which turns out to be a garage door, and are greeted by a pigeon named Hollywood. Her beak and eyelids are oddly deformed, and her feathers look cockeyed. Even I can tell there's something wrong with this bird.

Hollywood, it turns out, was the last surviving member of the inadvertent cast for Charlie Sheen's movie *No Code of Conduct,* which had the tagline "When crime is personal, there are no rules." One of the big finale scenes required blowing up a building on the outskirts of Phoenix. Although the production crew insisted they made their best effort to clear the abandoned structure of pigeons, more than 150 birds perished in the flames. Hollywood was the lone survivor. Roth nursed her back to health. "Back then she looked like a porcupine," Roth says. "She was burnt to hell."

Roth nuzzles Hollywood, cheek-to-cheek, beak-to-beak, as if she were some sort of winged puppy. She's a bit wary of me. "I don't know what I'd do without her," Roth says. "She sits right there and . . . well . . . as you can see, she greets me every day." Roth points to Hollywood's perch. I might have identified it myself. Perhaps it's the thick layer of dung dripping down the refrigerator door that's the dead giveaway. And yet it's plain that Hollywood has more than one favorite perch. Her dried shit is smeared across just about everything in the room—down shelves, closet doors, and an old washing machine. The room is littered with enormous piles of junk, and at one time or another Hollywood has made herself at home on each and every surface.

We walk farther into the house. The kitchen is also smothered in piles of bird droppings. Sweetie, a pigeon the size of a small turkey, is pacing back and forth on what used to be the kitchen counter.

Roth nuzzles her. "That's my girl. You're such a sweetie, aren't you?" He turns to face me. "If everybody could experience this kind of relationship with a bird, then we wouldn't have all the problems we have today with the pigeon haters . . . Pigeons can be funny, animated, and loyal like a dog. You'd be amazed."

The stove is covered in what looked like several years' worth of mail and, of course, bird shit. "Haven't used it in twenty years," Roth offers. In what once served as a living room are several cages housing rescued birds and their foot-high drip-drop turd castles. Roth senses my growing anguish, the fear in my eyes, the sweat on my upper lip. "What do you say we go grab some breakfast?" he offers cheerily. It's one-thirty P.M.

Outside, the sun shines, and I inhale deeply. We get into my car and Roth directs me onto the freeway. First we head east, then we head west, then we switch freeways. Roth doesn't get out much, and he is clearly a bit lost. When he was born, Phoenix was ninety-ninth among American cities, with a population of just over a hundred thousand and a footprint of just seventeen square miles. Phoenix now encompasses about five hundred square miles and has a population of 1.5 million. Due to a business-friendly environment, it is now the fifth largest city in America.

We make our way to a Phoenix landmark that happens to have been Roth's favorite place to eat as a kid—Bill Johnson's Big Apple. We're greeted by a hostess wearing a sheriff's badge on her western-style blouse. Sawdust covers the floor. Roth asks for the smoking section. "You betcha! Right this way!" she says.

Roth orders an omelet bursting at the seams with gooey cheese, and a large side of Tater Tots. He asks for a serving of barbecue sauce, homemade ranch dressing, and Thousand Island dressing for dipping. "That's why I wear these," Roth says in jest, pulling on his elastic shorts with his thumb. Although squeamish about ordering poultry in front of a bird activist, I request a grilled chicken garden salad with fat-free dressing. The waitress stares at me, mildly perplexed, and says she'll have to check on the dressing.

After "breakfast," Roth is in an adventurous mood. He suggests we search out rock doves in their "native habitat," a collection of sun-scorched rugged buttes on the outskirts of Phoenix. Once there, we park my rental car on the side of the road and hike into the desert, weaving past saguaro and cholla cacti, sage and creosote bushes. The mercury is approaching 100 degrees, and the buttes are about a mile distant. Roth stops for a cigarette. "Talk about out of shape. Damn! I'm even getting that secretary spread," he says, mopping his brow. Minutes later, he stops again, this time for a piss break.

I walk on ahead. Roth trails me by about a hundred feet, his black T-shirt hanging over his head, exposing his lily-white belly. He hams it up, moving his arms in the exaggerated motion of a speed walker. Once he catches up, I notice sweat gleaming from his every pore. We continue on, the sandy gravel crunching beneath our feet. Roth suddenly remembers the tape recorder in his pocket; he likes to tape every conversation. "Guess I might as well shut this off," he says. Out of curiosity, he rewinds it a few clicks and presses play. It's the amplified crunch of sandy gravel. He flips it off, and we are spared the sound of him pissing on the desert floor.

We approach the closest butte. I find a Boy Scout kerchief ring clasp but no sign of a pigeon, not even one shit-splattered rock. "I can't say I see any pigeons," I offer.

"No. Guess not," a disappointed Roth responds, "but this is their natural habitat . . ."

I shake my head and ponder the absurdity of the situation. Here we are, hiking in a desert that only a scorpion could find hospitable, looking for pigeons. Meanwhile, the pigeons are probably all downtown, gorging themselves on dropped doughnuts.

Back inside the air-conditioned car, Roth is more animated than I've seen him all morning. Physical exertion or not, he's plainly enjoying this diversion from his usual homebound routine. "You know, I should really thank you for getting me out of the house," he tells me. "I haven't taken a vacation since I visited Boston. And that was fifteen years ago."

Roth's earliest memory of pigeons is from when he was about eight years old. He and a friend were riding their banana-seat Sting-Rays through an alley when they saw some city police officers shooting pigeons on a church belfry. When he rode back through the alley a short time later, he saw a pigeon flopping around in its death throes. He picked up a big brick and smashed the bird's head to try and put it out of its misery. But it kept flopping around, and Roth raced home crying.

A few years later, an older kid started raising pigeons next door. Roth took a real liking to the birds, drawn to the unconditional love one receives from an animal. When his mother found out where he was spending his time, Roth says she made a big fuss about the pigeons being dirty and diseased and forced the neighbor to get rid of the birds. "I think that flipped a switch," Roth tells me. "I gave up on birds. I even started shooting animals. My friends and I would go into the desert and shoot lizards, snakes, whatever."

Years later as an adult Roth was shooting pigeons off his air-conditioning unit when he came across one bird that wouldn't be cowed. It was a baby pigeon, making those little peeping noises they make. Roth took pity and started feeding her. "I had two golden retrievers, so I just fed her dog kibble. She thrived on it." Roth named her PG, for Pretty Girl. Pretty soon PG was on Roth's shoulder, preening his hair, cooing in his ear, and eating kibble out of his shirt pocket.

A month later, he found her lying limply beneath his retrievers, dead. "It started a tremendous crying jag. I mean, blubbering that went on for hours. It was unbelievable. It must have been all that unresolved grief from so long ago . . . And that's when my life basically went to the birds."

Roth put out more and more food for a growing number of daily winged visitors. One day he came home and saw a dozen of them convulsing all over his yard and driveway. They had been poisoned by a pest control company somewhere else and had flown to his yard before the poison took effect. He frantically located an animal rehabber. The rehabber cut open the birds' crops and squeezed out the poisoned corn before flushing them with water. Several of the birds died, but two, Jackie and Normie, still live in Roth's living room.

"I thought, 'This can't be right. This can't be legal. It has to be stopped!'" Roth called the Arizona Game & Fish Department. He called the Humane Society. They all told him the same thing—it *was* legal to poison pigeons.

"That's how the whole thing started. It became my mission to make it illegal . . . I was an accidental activist. I never imagined one day it would consume my life. But seeing those birds convulsing . . . well, it was traumatic. You don't want to see those kinds of things happen to your friends."

Roth created the Urban Wildlife Society and became a point man for the Humane Society. He spent the next few years chasing down the complaints about pigeon poisonings and trying to educate landlords, business owners, and whoever would listen about more humane and more effective methods of bird control. He was a one-man educator and irritant.

"I learned just how difficult it is to change people's perceptions and just how entrenched bird poisoning was. The pest control companies have more money, and they continually run advertising campaigns for their services. And don't forget, Phoenix is the Wild West. It was 'If you don't like it, shoot it. Or poison it. Just kill it!' And after the killing's done, it's: 'Well, it needed killing.'"

Such must have been the attitude on a cool spring day in southern Ohio when a fourteen-year-old boy by the name of Press Clay Southworth spotted a strange bird eating grains of corn in his family's barnyard. He was familiar with local birds, but he'd never seen anything like this tall slender one. It looked roughly like a mourning dove but was about six inches longer and sported a crimson breast and fiery orange eyes.

As was common for his era, the boy found the animal so beautiful that he couldn't resist the urge to shoot it. He ran inside to grab a family shotgun and his mother's permission to use it. Back outside, he spied the prettily plumed bird resting high up in a tree. He aimed, fired, and down fell the last passenger pigeon witnessed in the wild. It was March 24, 1900.

"I . . . brought it down without much damage to its appearance," the shooter would brag to a newspaper reporter seven decades later. The family had the bird stuffed by a local taxidermist who used buttons for its eyes. Henceforth, the majestic bird would be known by the name "Buttons."

Fourteen years after Buttons' death, Martha, the last of her persecuted species, died a lonely death in captivity at the Cincinnati Zoo. A zoo employee found her lying motionless on the floor of her cage. She was twenty-nine. It's the only instance in history when the moment of a species extinction is known: September 1, 1914, at about one P.M. The world's last passenger pigeon was hardly a popular attraction, and news of the elderly bird's demise was lost amid the deafening guns of August and the start of World War I. Her corpse was packed into a three-hundred-pound block of ice and quietly shipped to the Smithsonian Institution for study and possible display.

It was a seemingly incomprehensible, not to mention heartbreaking, end to what was once the most populous bird in the Western Hemisphere and perhaps the planet. It is estimated that when Europeans first arrived in North America, there were as many as five billion passenger pigeons constituting as much as 40 percent of the continent's bird population.

A distant cousin of the rock dove, the passenger pigeon (*Ectopistes migratorius*) was famous for its giant migrations, or *passages* in French. Witnesses described skies darkening with millions of the large, colorful birds. They often flew in a formation one mile wide and up to three hundred miles long, an avian surge that lasted days. The sound of the birds passing overhead was often described as similar to hurricane-force winds or the roar of water bounding over Niagara Falls.

Stories of their abundance are legion and sound apocryphal, like that of the American buffalo. But their peculiar migrations were documented by thousands of witnesses, among them John Muir and John James Audubon. Muir described their all-day passage as like a "mighty river

in the sky, widening, contracting and descending like falls
. . ." Audubon recorded the following observation:

> In the autumn of 1813, I left my house . . . on the banks
> of the Ohio, on my way to Louisville. In passing . . . I
> observed the pigeons flying from northeast to southwest,
> in greater numbers than I thought I had ever seen them
> before . . . I traveled on, and still met more the farther I
> proceeded. The air was literally filled with pigeons; the
> light of noonday was obscured as by an eclipse, the dung
> fell in spots, not unlike melting flakes of snow; and the
> continued buzz of wings had a tendency to lull my senses
> to repose . . . Before sunset I reached Louisville . . . the
> pigeons were still passing in undiminished numbers, and
> continued to do so for three days in succession. The
> people were all in arms. The banks of the Ohio were
> crowded with men and boys, incessantly shooting at the
> pilgrims, which there flew lower as they passed the river.
> Multitudes were thus destroyed. For a week or more, the
> population fed on no other flesh than that of pigeons,
> and talked of nothing but pigeons.

The passenger pigeon made its home in the eastern half of North America, wintering in the American
South and migrating each year to New England, the upper
Midwest, and Canada to nest. These breeding grounds—
or pigeon cities—were enormous, often covering 750
square miles. The largest nesting ever witnessed covered
much of the southern two thirds of Wisconsin and parts
of neighboring Minnesota.

As its Latin name suggests, the passenger pigeon
was not only migratory but a wanderer as well. It traveled

to where the food was. In a single day, millions of the birds might fly as far as two hundred miles round-trip at an estimated 60 mph to retrieve a bounty of acorns, chestnuts, and beechnuts.

It was not uncommon for a hundred of the gregarious birds to share the same nesting tree, with dozens on the same branch. Thick and otherwise healthy hardwood branches routinely broke under their collective weight, crushing squabs and other birds below. Whole trees were seen to topple over, as if the area had been hit by a tornado. The nesting sites were so densely populated that the birds' incessant cooing was deafening. Audubon described the nesting grounds as

> a scene of uproar and confusion. I found it quite useless to speak, or even to shout to those persons who were nearest to me. Even the reports of the guns were seldom heard, and I was made aware of the firing only by seeing the shooters reloading.

It was a mixture of excesses—mostly greed and hatred—that doomed the passenger pigeon to extinction. First, the early American farmer shot them to protect his crops. An onslaught of the birds wreaked havoc with cultivated fields. Although pigeon droppings make a fine fertilizer, an excessive amount could prove ruinous. At roosting sites, piles of dung could be measured in feet. Second, an adult passenger pigeon was reasonably flavorsome, and a baby squab was downright succulent. As with the buffalo, the birds were overhunted for food and shot for sport.

Until the latter half of the nineteenth century, which witnessed the expansion of telegraph service and the railroads, the pigeon population could handle the assault. But these technologies aggressively intensified the slaughter. The telegraph enabled scouts to rapidly inform market hunters of a roosting site, and the trains made it possible to reach the sites quickly and then ship tens of millions of the birds as railway cargo to the big cities. Urbanites were fond of the bird's tender meat, as well as its colorful feathers for use as fashion accents.

Market hunters attacked the birds' nesting sites in search of the highly valued squab. A multitude of brutal methods were used, many of them employing a childlike simplicity. The birds were gunned down, trapped in nets, smoked out with fire and sulfur, or knocked out of their roosts with long poles. One day's haul could number in the tens of thousands. Far more birds were killed than could ever be used. Surplus birds were fed to hogs.

Equally important was the destruction of the passenger pigeon's habitat, as huge swaths were deforested to create millions more acres of arable land for an increasing number of European settlers. With each passing year, the bird found fewer places where it could roost en masse and comfortably propagate. To make matters worse, female passenger pigeons were not as fecund as their rock dove counterparts; they only laid one or two eggs a year, versus twelve to eighteen for a rock dove.

It took just twenty years, from 1870 to 1890, for the irreparable damage to occur. Billions of the mild-mannered birds were captured and killed, and the species couldn't compensate for the carnage. Once the population fell below a certain threshold, the passenger pigeon couldn't recover. Shortly before Martha's death, the Cincinnati Zoo offered a bounty of $1,000 to anyone who could find a mate for Martha. The award was never claimed.

The fate of the dodo bird was also sealed by human avarice and recklessness. Although an adult dodo stood three feet high, weighed as much as fifty pounds, and was incapable of flight, the bird was related to the passenger pigeon and the rock dove. It made its home in the dense forests and on the sandy beaches of Mauritius, a volcanic island in the Indian Ocean. With no natural predators, the peaceful bird lived what must have been a tranquil existence for a million years. The island was unknown by man until the sixteenth century.

The first recorded sighting of the big bird was in 1598. The word "dodo" is derived from *doudo,* an archaic Portuguese word for "simpleton." Apparently, the bird's unremarkable intelligence and comical appearance—a hooked beak, stout yellow legs, tiny wings, and an unruly tuft of curly feathers on its rump—had something to do with its naming.

The slow-moving birds were easy to hunt—one had only to approach it with a stout club—and made for tolerable, if not tasty, eating to hungry Dutch and Portuguese sailors. An even greater threat was the introduction of pigs, rats, and monkeys that plundered the bird's nests, which lay exposed on the forest floor. Add deforestation to the mix, and it's easy to see how the clumsy, affable bird met its demise.

The last confirmed dodo sighting was by a shipwrecked mariner in 1681. It took just eighty-three years to obliterate the species.

The netting and electric wires are still firmly in place ten years later at the Maricopa County jail, as if they had just been installed. Where there were once more than a thousand pigeons, there are now none. Standing outside the building with me, Roth is clearly filled with pride and vindication. A big smile broadens across his face.

"This was a defining incident. This one incident had a ripple effect that saved countless birds' lives . . . What we accomplished at this jail established a precedent for other governments to follow. The county protected their other buildings this way, and soon the city and the state followed suit. This is a total success story."

However, to Roth's dismay, bird poisoning remains legal in Arizona. "It should fall under the animal cruelty laws, but there's still so much resistance," he adds. "Changing that law has become mission impossible. Which is sad. Once you get to know pigeons, it's like poisoning children."

The biggest myth he continually confronts is one propagated by the pest control companies—that pigeons carry dozens of deadly and contagious diseases. "It's just a big scare tactic . . . they stigmatize pigeons to make money."

For evidence, Roth disseminates information from the federal Centers for Disease Control in Atlanta ("diseases associated with [pigeons] present little risk to people") and the Arizona Department of Health Services ("At present, we do not have any documented human cases of disease which have been definitively linked to outdoor pigeons or pigeon droppings . . . Our case investigation data gathered so far would suggest that pigeons are not significant as a cause of human disease in Arizona").

It's difficult to argue against Roth's assertions. When it comes to pigeon control, he's the voice of reason and research. Listening to him is like listening to a dynamic if absentminded college professor—he's done his homework. His delivery is surprisingly compelling and authoritative yet unemotional. After all, he won the prison debate by arguing fiscal responsibility.

Back at his house, Roth walks me over to two home-made tombstones, one for a bird named Tux and another for Pretty Girl. The latter reads: "A most rare, loving and trusting pet. One in a million among pigeons. Died August 4, 1990."

A grave for the famed Tootsie is nowhere to be found. "I was just way too upset," Roth says. "I let the vet take care of it. I didn't even want to know what happened to her afterwards. It was probably just 'froze and dispose.' Tootsie was special. Uncommonly special."

Roth tells me he is particularly sickened by anything that causes the premature death of a pigeon. His response to dove hunting? "Taking a life for a spoonful of meat? C'mon." Dining on squab? "That's like Jeffrey Dahmer eating your kid." He is appalled by pigeon-related hobbies as well, including the seemingly harmless pursuit of breeding fancy pigeons, which he terms "eugenics, pure and simple." He considers pigeon racing exploitative of the animal's compulsion to return home and compares it to "kidnapping in reverse." Racers, he says, are gamblers who deliberately place their birds in harm's way and routinely push them to utter exhaustion for financial gain. "Why is that okay?"

Back inside, we hack our way through the debris like jungle explorers. Roth introduces me to several more of his rescues. They are Jimmy (as in Durante), a pied peach-faced lovebird with a big schnozzle; Pookie Flip (aka Flippie Pook) and Myrtle, two white-winged doves;

Tippy, a big fat hen-like pigeon; and three mourning doves, Love Dove, Squiggy, and Sprinky. Sprinky is so named because his head moves in a repetitive staccato fashion, much like an automated lawn sprinkler.

Roth wants to show me some videotapes in his living room of news stories that he helped get on-air. There's furniture everywhere, but it's covered with old computer parts, mail, aged newspapers, empty potato chip bags, pigeon droppings, and dust. Roth finds me a folding chair and sets it down in front of a television balanced precariously atop a chest-high ten-foot-long pile of more junk in the middle of the room. "I used to spend more time in here," he says.

Ten minutes later, he finds the VHS tape he was looking for and blows a quarter inch of dust off the jacket. "Guess this hasn't been looked at for a while." The newscast, an investigative piece about pigeon shoots, is several years old. Roth furtively shot the video of marksmen using live pigeons as clay targets. He passed the video on to the local network affiliates, who all ran with it. The raw video still riles him. "Those poor birds. Some of them are just babies. Where's the challenge? You call this sporting? Can you believe they give out ribbons for this?"

We run through endless more stories with pigeons as news pegs. There's one about a pet bird killed by pigeon poison and another with apartment residents in an uproar about suffering pigeons flopping on their lawn. "I've placed more than a hundred stories on TV," Roth says. "But we're talking over the course of sixteen years."

On our way outside to Roth's backyard aviary, we pass a wall lined with large empty boxes, the remnants of what passes for nutrition in Roth's cloistered world. Just about everything he eats is microwaved. I see several empty cases from iced honey buns, Ritz crackers, and, to my surprise, corn dogs and chicken chimichangas. "Sometimes my neighbors buy something at Costco that they don't particularly like, so they give it to me to eat. I don't feel like I'm impacting the animal—it was headed for the trash anyway. Look, I'm not perfect, but I think my footprint is pretty small."

Just around the corner is Roth's headquarters, where he says he spends a hundred hours a week working to save pigeons, stopping only to use the bathroom and the microwave. The desk is covered with a jumble of parts cannibalized from donated computers. The six hard drives that he cobbled together hold a respectable terabyte of information. He's very proud of the number of visitors to his Web site—just under a million hits a year.

Outside, Roth keeps two small aviaries for sixty rescued birds. The structures are also encrusted in crud. Roth explains that the feces are not health hazards. "Their poop is clean. I've had it tested." Nevertheless, I figure that being around that much crap can't be good for anyone's health, and I keep a safe distance.

Roth also has large blocks of birdseed and containers of water on his lawn. Several hundred pigeons visit daily, though only a few dozen spend the night. "Basically, this is a loafing site," he says. "It's like the pigeon version of *Cheers*. I keep them out of trouble here, out of harm's way."

We go back inside, and Roth finally addresses the elephant in the room—his chaos theory of household maintenance. "Don't think any of this is lost on me," he says. "I just choose to ignore it. How many hours does it take to clean a house every week? Two? Three? Now spread that out over sixteen years. Imagine how many more birds I have saved because of the extra time I could devote to their cause."

But how long does he see himself living like this?

"I'm not sure I even enjoy it anymore. I don't have the same vitality that I used to have. I don't feel that I'm as effective. But I can't stop advocating for pigeons. Trying to stop feels worse than doing it. I tried it once on the recommendation of a therapist. But I couldn't.

"The need I have to continue is visceral. Ever have a bad breakup and your heart hurts so much that you don't think the hurt will ever stop? That's what it's like. I hurt when they hurt. What can I say? I suffer from terminal empathy." Roth makes a sweeping gesture of the room. "Just look at my cage."

As Roth takes his pigeon campaign worldwide through the Internet and e-mail—he has scuttled plans for pigeon extermination in cities all across the country—his greatest challenge is right down the street. The neighbor is clearly not a pigeon lover. Roth says the man used to leave beheaded birds outside Roth's front door. "I see this cruel streak all the time when it comes to pigeons," Roth tells me. "Pigeons bring out extremes in the human spectrum."

After a series of inconclusive court battles, the two neighbors have harbored a cold peace for the past twelve years. We drove past the man in the neighborhood earlier in the day. Roth tried to hide his face but ended up waving meekly as we sped off. Later, when we are standing on the sidewalk, Roth asks me to speak in a whisper. "I don't want anything to set him off. When he gets angry, he starts killing birds."

Roth's neighbor, I soon find, is not alone. Some people like pigeons. But pigeons also piss a lot of people off. I decide there's no better laboratory than New York City—"the world's capital"—for studying this dichotomy.

8

Flying Rats

MOST DENIZENS OF NEW YORK DESCRIBE THEIR CITY'S pigeons alternately as "dirty," "filthy," and "disease-ridden." Although pigeons attempt to groom themselves daily, they do in fact poo in their own nests. Combine that with the perilous life of scavenging in a grimy, sooty city, and you can understand why some city pigeons look less than manicured. One urban aphorism often applied to the rock dove is the regrettable moniker "rats with wings."

Although he probably did not invent the slur, Woody Allen popularized it in his 1980 movie *Stardust Memories* when he panicked at the sight of a pigeon in his apartment: "It's not pretty at all. They're, they're, they're rats with wings! . . . It's probably one of those killer pigeons . . . You see? It's got a swastika under its wings."

Although a mere one-liner in just one of Allen's many movies, it was nevertheless the shot heard 'round the world, one that put pigeons and their perches in the cultural crosshairs. Urban pigeon haters finally had a rallying cry. Pigeons, of course, are not rodents and have few similarities to them besides. The only thing they may have in common, in addition to both being vertebrates, is their hankering for human leftovers and a tendency to live in large urban colonies. (No, pigeons do not carry plague.) Combine Allen's slur with Tom Lehrer's 1959 satirical song "Poisoning Pigeons in the Park," in which he waxes poetic about feeding them cyanide-coated peanuts, and you can see why these birds are badly in need of a public relations makeover. Hatred of pigeons has become so fanatical that one resident of New York City recently published a book graphically outlining 101 ways to kill a pigeon, including: "Grab a pigeon by the head. Twist until you hear a 'pop.' Grab another bird and repeat."

It's difficult to tell if it's the pigeons or their excrement that truly pisses people off. After all, it's the droppings, not the pigeons, that blanket cities with unsightly noxious splatter. And it's their acidic dung that eats through stone and metal, corroding buildings, monuments, and (gasp!) automobile paint. It's also fertile ground for dangerous parasites and infectious bacteria.

Yet there was a time when pigeon droppings were considered a semiprecious commodity. In ancient Egypt, they were a highly prized manure that worked agricultural wonders because of a high nitrogen content. For centuries in England, only the wealthy were allowed to raise pigeons for food, and the feces were declared property of the crown. The valuable dung was used to manufacture saltpeter, a critical ingredient for making gunpowder.

Far from being a carefully guarded royal wonder, pigeon dung is now considered a health hazard and aesthetic nuisance. It's not that the feral pigeon is a particularly prodigious pooer. It's just that, unlike most birds, it congregates in large gregarious flocks that call our cities their home. Pigeons are attracted to the sight of other pigeons, and their droppings rapidly accumulate, much like bats and guano.

As their name suggests, feral pigeons were once domestic, just like wild ponies or the parrots of Telegraph Hill. They are dovecote escapees and the descendants of escapees that have flown the coop. As sport racing increased in popularity, many homers either lost their way or called it quits and joined these feral flocks. If you look closely at the pigeons in your park, you just might see one of them wearing a racing band around its leg.

These pigeons are survivors and have done remarkably well for themselves. They are particularly well adapted to urban living. Buildings provide them with plenty of nooks and crannies for nesting, and humans' pathological carelessness with food provides them sustenance. Bagels, doughnuts, pizza crusts are the mainstay of a modern feral pigeon's diet. Despised for the messes they leave behind, these birds actually act as spontaneous street cleaners picking up after human litterbugs.

Since the beginning of the industrial revolution, humans have flocked to cities, and as we go, so go the feral pigeons. They remain attracted to us and follow us wherever we go. To a pigeon, more people mean more buildings and more scraps of food. Biologists term this behavior *commensal*, from the Latin "com mensa," meaning to share a table. Rock doves thrive in these conditions. But the more they prosper, the more they propagate, and the more they bombard us with their excrement. The average pigeon produces over twenty-five pounds of droppings a year. At some urban nesting sites, the accumulated crap can be measured in tons.

As our culture becomes increasingly hygienic, we have less tolerance for this sort of mess. What consumer would eat at a restaurant or shop at a market whose awnings were splattered with dung? What employee wants to breathe in air from a rooftop ventilation system that's home to dozens of roosting pigeons? The peaceful coexistence between man and pigeon, which lasted for thousands of years, has deteriorated into a war of attrition. The urban pigeon, regardless of its remarkable past and incredible physiology, is now considered a feathered outlaw.

The generals and foot soldiers in this pigeon war are the owners and employees of the multibillion-dollar bird control industry. As you might expect, they have few kind words for the rock dove. According to many in the pest control industry, the rock dove is nothing more than a filthy, bacteria-ridden, disease-carrying vermin with absolutely no redeeming qualities. If the industry could pin AIDS and bubonic plague on the pigeon, they'd do so in a New York minute.

They've helped foster an environment where, for the first time in human history, pigeons are routinely ridiculed, vilified, and persecuted. The pigeon hasn't changed one iota, but after decades of ridicule and bad press, the public's perception of the bird has gone from admiration for its unique history to fear and disgust.

When small outbreaks of West Nile Virus whipped the American public into a near-frenzy not long ago, it was a boon for the pigeon control industry. Some saw their business nearly triple. Lost in the shuffle was the fact that pigeons don't transmit West Nile Virus; mosquitoes do. Pigeons don't carry the virus, either, because their body temperature is too high to host the bacteria. Further studies have shown pigeons to be either resistant or minimally susceptible to avian influenza as well.

Here's the poop on pigeons: their droppings can be linked to more than sixty communicable (bacterial and viral) diseases, but then again, so can yours. Yes, they *can* pose a health risk, but one that is comparable to cleaning out Whisker's litter box. Cat feces can contain parasites that cause toxoplasmosis, a disease that can result in neurological damage. Feral pigeons are more susceptible to these diseases than racing and show pigeons, which are typically kept in cleaned and maintained backyard coops.

The two diseases most commonly associated with pigeon dung are histoplasmosis, which attacks the lungs, and cryptococcosis, which causes meningitis and encephalitis. It's important to emphasize that neither disease is *carried* by pigeons. Rather, they are caused by fungi that exist all around us, particularly in soil. Pigeon dung happens to be an attractive breeding ground for these fungal spores because it is highly acidic and acts as a fertilizer. Chicken shit, by comparison, rapidly becomes alkaline and thus fungus-unfriendly.

There is no ironclad evidence that pigeons spread disease to humans. However, Dr. Arturo Casadevall, director of the Division of Infectious Diseases at Manhattan's Albert Einstein College of Medicine, says he suspects that people with weakened immune systems are at risk around pigeon feces.

Casadevall is one of the world's foremost experts in pigeon poop, an area of study that he characterizes as "not particularly crowded." His work with AIDS patients suffering from cryptococcosis suggests that they may have inhaled the spores in the vicinity of roosting city pigeons. "The vast majority of people will never get sick," Casadevall says. "But if you're one of the unlucky few . . ."

The easiest way to get sick from pigeon excrement is from cleaning it out of an unventilated space, such as an attic. When you disturb the feces, it will turn to dust if already dry, and the spores will dangle in the air. Breathing in large quantities of doo-doo dust is not a recommended activity, which is why professional bird shit removers wet the droppings first, ventilate the area, and wear respirators.

But picking on pigeons is unwarranted, Casadevall warns. "Pigeons are no different than other animals. When it comes to spreading disease, they don't stand out. Dogs can have worms; bats, rabies; cats, toxoplasmosis . . . We're exposed to microbes everywhere. You can get diseases from any animal, even a cockatoo. To single out pigeons is unfair."

Dr. Nina Marano, an epidemiologist with the Centers for Disease Control in Atlanta, agrees. "Pigeons are no more filthy than any other wild bird or animal. The problem is that they congregate very near to us and in large numbers." Pigeon overcrowding leads to large concentrated quantities of feces. The accumulation in an area highly trafficked by pedestrians is not something health officials are likely to endorse.

Early attempts at pigeon control usually involved picking off the birds one by one with a rifle. Although cruel and ineffective, this method is still in use today. The first so-called humane bird control product to be commercially manufactured was developed in 1950 in the American Midwest. Invented by a lawyer with an entrepreneurial drive, Nixalite is the spiky metal stuff you see on many city ledges. You'll even find it on top of the Alaska pipeline and on Coast Guard buoys out at sea. It's still in use, although more effective variations, with fewer piercingly sharp needles, have also been developed. Another humane favorite is netting draped tightly over potential pigeon perches.

Succeeding decades saw an alarming rise in cruel and desperate products and practices. Ledges were covered in chemical gels that either irritated the birds' feet or released strychnine into their bloodstream. Other entrepreneurs developed high-voltage platforms that electrocuted any bird landing on them. Some of these products have been banned and are no longer in use.

One product still used in many cities is Avitrol, a pesticide-laden bird food developed by a man whose last name is Swindle. Approved for use by the United States government, Avitrol is designed to bait and disorient a small portion of a flock. Other pigeons in the flock are supposed to flee after seeing the poisoned birds in distress. But more often than not, Avitrol is used as an avicide. As Avitrol's own literature states, "Dead or reacting birds in public areas may be an alarming sight to the general public. It is best to gather and dispose of dead birds regularly, especially if adverse public reaction is anticipated."

Not only are avicides cruel, they're also indiscriminate. So-called desirable birds are lured to their last meal as well. These poisoned birds make for easy prey and can end up in the stomachs of endangered species, such as the peregrine falcon.

While the bird control industry has its share of warped entrepreneurs who malign pigeons and busy themselves devising death traps, the industry has its fair share of goofy suburban warriors and their even sillier slogans ("We're number one at number two!"). Jack Wagner, a bird control expert with an irreverent take on his profession, is a prime example. He's been in business for twenty-five years and has used just about every product out there.

A roofer by trade, Wagner fell into bird control by accident. While he was on the job in Washington, D.C., more and more clients asked him for help with roosting pigeons. At the time, bird control experts were few and far between, so Jack experimented and improvised with whatever products existed.

One of his first clients was a drugstore on Dupont Circle. Jack improvised an electrical wiring system and installed it while hanging precariously from ropes and scaffolding. When he saw the flock leave the drugstore only to roost on the building right next door, Jack knew he was on to something. He dropped roofing and took up bird control full-time.

"My job involves architecture and biology," Jack tells me. "How fascinating is that? I get paid to outwit nature but not harm it, and to make sure that it is done in an architecturally correct way. In a sense, I'm an artist, mechanic, and biologist."

Jack named his new company BirdBusters (after the then recently released *Ghostbusters*) and was the first bird control expert to acquire an 800 number (1-800-NO-BIRDS). His flamboyant style attracted business from across the country and even the world. Not only has he pigeon-proofed sections of the U.S. Capitol, his work has taken him to the Sudan, the United Arab Emirates, Alaska, Hong Kong, and the Caribbean. "Pigeons are a problem everywhere. They're the mainstay of the bird control industry. If my business were a gas station, they'd be the pump: steady, steady, steady." (Woodpeckers, however, are fast pushing pigeons out of their first place perch. Says Jack, "They're like a carpenter on speed with an ax.")

Jack has mixed feelings about pigeons. On one hand, he calls them disgusting birds that nest in their own crap. Conversely, he sees them as harmless loafers that have survived millions of years of evolution only to be hounded by modern humans. "Sure, they'll crap on your birthday cake, but they're pacifists," Jack says. "They don't mean any harm. They just want to eat and hang out."

Ridding an area of pigeons does have some painful but beneficial consequences, such as leaving more food for smaller birds. "It's sort of like *Sophie's Choice*—for every pigeon and starling I knock off, a sparrow or songbird lives."

Jack says he's disappointed with nearly every product he's used against pigeons. He's tried speakers that emit avian distress signals; deterrent gels ("We sell bird gel remover; that's how bad it is"); bird spikes ("You know how a Hindu can sit on a bed of nails? Well, pigeons can too"); traps employed for later release ("They're not called *homing* pigeons for nothing"); lasers; and avicides ("A bunch of lies. Distress signal? Baloney. They're dying: That's the distress signal. It's poison"). Fake owls are so lame, they're a standing joke in the business.

These days Jack is touting something called the Firefly, a six-inch wavy length of reflective plastic that produces glare. He strings them from buildings and swears by the results. "It truly affects their vision. They stay away!"

David Kane, who runs a New York outfit called Bye Bye Birdie, is a good friend of Jack's but thinks Jack has gone off the deep end with this Firefly business. David is a traditionalist. He believes that the only way to rid a building of pigeons is to wrap it in spikes, electrical wires, and netting. In the back of his maroon Buick LeSabre, he keeps a wooden box displaying the tricks of his trade, with names like Bird Coil, Flex-track, and StealthNet, "a poly netting with a forty-four-pound breaking point." It's this display and the knowledge behind it that differentiate David from the small-timers, he says. "All those guys know is spikes. That's it."

Although he works on jobs as big as airports and entire college campuses, today he's tooling around Brooklyn with a detailed street map, writing up estimates for small residential jobs. He's continually on his cell phone, calling clients. "Hi, I'm David Kane from Bye Bye Birdie. Rich from Queensway Extermination suggested I give you a call. Where's the problem? On the front of the building? I'll be by to take a look."

After a succession of these calls, David turns to me in frustration. "These little jobs? I'm over it. I basically do them as favors for people I know. Most of these customers don't want to spend the kind of money it takes to get rid of pigeons anyway. They think it's just a matter of putting up a fake owl. But when they see us show up at the crack of dawn with a sixty-foot boom truck, they know it's serious business."

The jobs David dislikes even more are when he and his employees spend a night in a high-ceilinged big-box store trying to capture a stray bird with big nets hanging from forty-foot extension poles. "You have to figure out the bird's flight pattern, agitate it with a laser, and then try to catch it in these giant nets. But you're always taking the nets back down and moving them again and again. It's a monotonous, horrible job. Nobody wants it." It once took four nights and $7,000 in labor to capture a little sparrow that resorted to hiding under the store's aisles to evade capture.

When we arrive on a job, David takes out a sketch-book and a measuring tape and starts writing the estimate. The first thing he does is look down at the pavement for the telltale splatters of bird shit. Only then does he look up at a building's ledges and cornices. I watch as a pigeon poops on the hood of David's car and another soils his light green oxford, a sure sign that he spends his days pursuing pigeons.

After years of practice, David can spot the problem in minutes, if not seconds. He usually recommends that the owner pigeon-proof the second to fifth floors of a building, where pigeons tend to roost on ledges, cornices, and under air-conditioning units. Pigeons favor these heights because they're elevated enough to offer protection from pedestrians, but not so high as to distance the birds from their sidewalk food source (which is why you're unlikely to see a pigeon on top of the Empire State Building).

When estimating a job, David ranks the degree of pigeon infiltration and puts it in one of three categories: low-, medium-, and high-pressure. A low-pressure job consists of a smattering of pigeons routinely sunning themselves on a comfortable southern-facing ledge. A simple application of spikes and coils will do the trick. A medium-pressure job means the birds are hanging out because there's a nearby food source such as a bus stop where people drop their half-eaten bagels before boarding. This density can require electrical work.

A high-pressure job denotes an area where the pigeons aren't just loafing or eating but also nesting. "That's the hardest pressure to eliminate," David explains to me. Pigeons don't like to move. Once they're born in a place, that's it, they're committed for life. They're staying no matter what and will build a nest on top of spikes if they have to. The only way to keep them away is total exclusion. And that's what netting is for. "If nothing else, pigeons are persistent, and there's plenty of them," David says. "They're my bread and butter."

Unlike Jack, David started in pest control before specializing in bird control, and he says, "I think there's an untapped market in geese." So his next business project will be tackling the geese that congregate at corporate parks and crap all over the expansive lawns.

As Jack and David can attest, bird control is an addictive and obsessive career. On a trip to Paris with his wife, David visited the Louvre. Rather than admiring the *Mona Lisa* with his wife, he found his eyes wandering to an outside ledge covered in bird wire. "I can't help it. It's my business. It's what I do."

On his way to another estimate, David makes a short detour and parks his car across the street from the Brooklyn Museum of Art. He aims binoculars at the building's enormous classical pediment and Ionic columns. A competitor recently installed netting to protect the ornate facade from pigeons.

"Wow. Look at that. You can't even see the netting. It's so taut the pigeons probably bounce off it. Now, that's something to be proud of."

★ ★ ★

As honest bird control experts will tell you, their product is at best a temporary solution. Total exclusion works, but it protects only one physical location. The birds just relocate to another roost nearby. Ask David Kane what he does for a living, and he'll tell you he's in the bird relocation business.

You can't wrap an entire city in netting. So what's a city to do? Sadly, most still depend on the most primitive of methods—killing pigeons. It's an ineffective method, and most pest control companies know this, but they continue to push these profitable services anyway.

To howls of protest from pigeon lovers and animal-rights activists, the mayor of London, Ken Livingstone, recently declared war on the pigeons of Trafalgar Square, using a brutal mixture of lethal and nonlethal methods. He shut down a vendor whose family had sold birdseed to tourists since World War II, banned the feeding of pigeons altogether, and hired a falconer to patrol the square daily. But it's not Lord Nelson's column or the National Gallery alone that attract flocks of tourists to Trafalgar Square, it's also the birds. Days before I visited the square to gauge the situation for myself, Paris Hilton made a splash when police issued her a $100 summons for feeding the birds. "But I just love feeding the pigeons in Trafalgar Square," she said. "I could do it forever. I even prefer it to going shopping."

With fewer pigeons visible Livingstone is seemingly winning the Battle of Trafalgar Square, but for how long and at what cost? Using falconry for pigeon control is cruel as well as unsustainable: pigeons return the minute the falconer leaves. And the sight of a falcon ferociously dining on a splayed pigeon is traumatic for the public, especially children. A policy built on hatred is hardly a recipe for success, and it has unfortunately blinded Livingstone to the basic facts of bird control. Sadly, the mayor of Venice is considering similar measures to rid St. Mark's Square of pigeons.

A Swiss biologist by the name of Daniel Haag-Wackernagel has spent over a decade studying pigeon populations and how to regulate them in an urban setting. His work turned many basic assumptions upside down. First, killing birds only *increases* the size of a flock. The loss of life means less competition and more food for the rest of the flock. That, in turn, means that a new generation of young birds is more likely to survive.

Haag-Wackernagel surmised that the key to controlling a pigeon population was food. Pigeons breed only when there's food available. When food is overly bountiful, as was the case at Trafalgar Square, pigeons will mate as often as possible, up to six times a year. When food is scarce, the mating routine drops dramatically, because pigeons must spend their time anxiously foraging for food.

Haag-Wackernagel used the streets of Basel as his laboratory. Between 1961 and 1985, marksmen hired by the city killed approximately one hundred thousand pigeons. But the pigeon population grew over this time. The first thing Haag-Wackernagel did was to launch a civic campaign to educate the public about pigeon feeding. Overfeeding, he explained, is an artificial intervention in a city's ecosystem. It leads to overpopulation and overcrowding, which stress a flock and encourage sickness and disease. In effect, Haag-Wackernagel declared, overfeeding pigeons is tantamount to animal cruelty.

Next Haag-Wackernagel set up clean lofts at hidden locations around the city and encouraged the pigeons to nest there, in effect returning the birds to the dovecotes where they originated centuries ago. Volunteers visited the lofts weekly to leave feed and clean up after the birds and regularly replaced their eggs with wooden or plastic facsimiles.

Within four years, Basel's pigeon population was reduced by 50 percent. Interestingly, the city's largest bird control company saw its sales drop by an astonishing two thirds during the same period. Haag-Wackernagel proved that pigeon populations, unlike rats, really could be controlled, and humanely. And as flocks thin, hatred for the bird subsides. It's not the bird itself that annoys most people, it's the *number* of them.

A British nonprofit organization called the Pigeon Control Advisory Service (PiCAS) developed a similar strategy that has shown impressive results. At one of its projects, a public hospital in Nottingham, PiCAS reduced the bird population by 50 percent in under a year.

PiCAS began as the brainchild of Guy Merchant, a willowy man in his fifties who has dedicated his life to educating the public about humane and effective urban pigeon control. He has consulted for cities halfway around the globe and never charges a fee for his services.

"We are the only independent source of unbiased information out there," Guy says. "By comparison, the pest control industries are only motivated by greed. They invest millions of dollars each year on anti-pigeon propaganda and misinformation. It's entirely unethical. In fact, there are no ethics involved at all. Believe you me, the world hates pigeons because of them."

I met with Guy over a cup of coffee at his tidy home in Cambridgeshire. Few people in the world have dedicated their lives so totally to pigeons, with the possible exception of Dave Roth in Phoenix. Like Roth, he basically *is* the organization.

"I care about all birds, but the plight of the feral pigeon is far worse than the others," Guy says. "They are abused and tortured more than any other bird, and usually for profit. It just sticks in my throat. They're the ultimate underdog." He works 365 days a year to help pigeons, including every Christmas for over thirty years. "For better or worse, I live, eat—figuratively—and sleep pigeons." He blames a recent stroke on his obsessive work habits, but it hasn't slowed him down.

A trained bird rehabilitator, Guy started PiCAS three decades ago, after treating an onslaught of sick and dying pigeons—the result of lethal bird control methods. "Once I learned how appalling, cruel, and ineffective those methods were, I had to come up with a solution. I had no choice but to dedicate my life to it. That's what started PiCAS—the massive buildup of dead and dying pigeons."

Guy says the biggest hurdle of any urban pigeon campaign is convincing the skeptical public to limit how much they feed the city's birds. Residents often fear the birds will starve and complain that they miss their relaxing daily routine of bird feeding. To combat this compulsion, PiCAS recommends building attractive lofts and designating them as places where feeding is encouraged. Some cities have created contests in which artists and architects design the lofts, which double as public art. PiCAS also recommends a thorough bird-proofing of public buildings where the birds used to make their homes, to ensure that they don't return.

The Basel/PiCAS models have been embraced by many cities in Europe. Visiting Aachen, in Germany, I was amazed at how unobtrusive the pigeons were. Instead of foraging for scraps in the city center, they happily loafed at well-maintained lofts circling the city. City residents had reached a détente with their feathered friends.

Compulsive feeding by certain individuals remains the biggest threat to the European model. Compulsive feeders will dodge fines, absorb public humiliation, and even resort to secret night feedings to avoid detection. "A small number of persistent and deliberate feeders are wholly responsible for the pigeon problem throughout the world," says Guy. "They *are* the pigeon problem. Pigeons overbreed when people overfeed. There is no other explanation."

According to Guy, regardless of where they live, compulsive feeders share similar quirky personality traits and slip into the obsession in nearly identical ways. "They're a strange bunch, extremely eccentric." Although compulsive feeders view themselves as charitable, Guy thinks them selfish. It's not enough to simply feed the pigeons, he says. All that does is burden everyone else with cleaning up the resulting mess.

Manhattan is home to countless unusual and lonely characters who seek solace by feeding pigeons from park benches. It's a classic New York preoccupation, practiced by the elderly, the unemployed, the curious, the melancholy, and the lonely. After all, if the human condition is ultimately to be alone, then why not let a few pigeons help us pass the time?

Some of these folks have routinely fed pigeons for years, if not decades. But when it comes to compulsive feeding, they can't outshine the likes of Sally Bananas and Anna Dove.

Sally, an elderly but energetic woman with a fondness for tight leggings, floppy hats, and oversize sunglasses, changed her last name to Bananas in honor of her poodle, Charlie Bananas. After a long life, Charlie is now in doggy heaven, but Sally still gets his mail (from Victoria's Secret, nonetheless) and telemarketing calls (the phone is in his name). "I tell them he's traveling in Brazil," she tells me. "That usually shuts them up."

Charlie Bananas was part of Sally's now-deceased Banana Gang, an entity that she says she had hoped to legally incorporate. There was also Sandy-of-Oz (with hyphens, please) and little José Caliente, who served as the "caboose of the gang." And there were three cats: Subway Red, Willie Whiskers, and Choo-Choo. Sally treated Charlie to drinks at the Waldorf-Astoria and says the whole gang joined her for a cruise on the *QE2*. Sally's dream of marching down the Champs Élysées with the whole Banana gang was thwarted by Charlie's untimely passing.

Sally says she prefers the company of animals to humans. "If a dog ran for president, I'd vote for him," she says. "I've lost faith in the human race." After the passing of the Banana Gang, Sally has lived alone. She considers the neighborhood pigeons her family now. Most days Sally lugs forty to fifty pounds of birdseed around her Upper East Side neighborhood and hastily spills large quantities of it at her "usual spots." It's become a habit, she readily admits, "because the birds need" her.

"They know me," she says of her pigeons. "No matter how I'm dressed, they know who I am. And they're always so hungry, the poor darlings. We've taken away their habitat. Imagine if you had to hunt around for a seed to survive. Remember, every animal was once a mother's child."

Sally Bananas is friends with Anna Dove, whose name used to be Augusta Kugelmas. She changed her name in honor of her pet pigeon Lucie-Dove. It occurs to me that the names are a bit too perfect and the women perhaps prefer the use of animal-friendly pseudonyms— noms de guerre, if you will—when interacting with the outside world. Anna lives alone with her menagerie of doves, parakeets, parrots, finches, and a rabbit. She runs a club that organizes bird playdates, although she confesses that she doesn't enjoy working with other people and prefers to keep to herself.

A few years ago she was arrested for allegedly assaulting a Parks Department volunteer who insisted that Anna (then Augusta) stop feeding the pigeons. The volunteer claimed it was illegal. Anna insists the volunteer was "a bitch with Mafioso ties" and that she merely threw birdseed at the woman to protect herself. "She grabbed my bag of food," Anna recalls. "There was . . . a scuffle." The charges were dropped, but not before the quintessentially New York story made it onto the pages of the city's dailies and weeklies: WOMAN ARRESTED FOR FEEDING PIGEONS!

Anna used the publicity to form a pigeon club of irate citizens looking to defend their right to feed pigeons.

The group met at a local bagel shop but eventually disbanded over internal squabbling. "We discussed things like how we should feed the pigeons and what to do about people that harass us. But nothing ever got accomplished. It became all about ego and who was in charge of the group."

Although pigeon feeding is illegal in some cities, such as San Francisco, it remains legal in New York City. A casualty of bureaucratic logic, pigeon feeding falls under the jurisdiction of the city's Department of Health, which issues summonses only if the feeding creates a nuisance condition—basically, if it attracts rats.

Anna tells me that she sympathizes with the city's concern about rats. This year she found mice in her apartment and was, in her words, "devastated to the point that I could not live my life." She removed all sources of food from her apartment, even her refrigerator and stove, and slept in the hallway a couple of nights. She knew better than to ask her landlord for help. Earlier, when the ceiling above her bed had erupted with several gallons of water from burst pipes, he suggested she sleep on the couch.

Anna was in the news again when she posted a $10,000 reward for a missing exotic parrot she was tending. Against the owner's wishes, Anna brought the bird down to the lobby to get some fresh air, and the parrot promptly escaped. (It was later recovered, unharmed.)

When it comes to feeding pigeons, Anna says she has been pushed, shoved, berated, and threatened by fellow pedestrians. But she refuses to back down. "I've taken a stand," she says. "If you wanna stop me, go buy a gun and shoot me, because that's what it's going to take."

One of her favorite stories is about a security guard who used to work just outside her building. One day he confronted her for feeding a peanut to a squirrel. "He tells me he's going to report me and starts shouting into his walkie-talkie for backup. All because I was feeding a squirrel! Can you believe it? What a sick bastard. Well, later on I found out that he dropped dead the very next day. You know what I said? 'Good, that's one less person I have to worry about.' Now I feed ten squirrels with a whole bag of nuts. And you know what? Nobody says a word."

I spent a sunny afternoon accompanying the two ladies on their feeding safari. It proved a far more difficult undertaking than I had imagined. Both women had the unnerving ability to speak to me at the exact same time, one in each ear. Sally compulsively interrupted Anna, and Anna just kept right on talking (as did Sally).

Our expedition begins outside a coffee shop on First Avenue, along Sally's main route. It starts with her giving a young couple a lecture about tying their dog to a tree while they run in for a cup of coffee. "It's very dangerous," she says. "It's a hot sun. Many dogs are stolen. It's not safe, not safe at all. There's shade under that tree over there, but that's where two little puppies got killed." At first friendly, the couple eventually stare at Sally blankly before walking to another coffee shop.

Meanwhile, Anna is busy feeding sparrows bread crumbs between her own bites. "Today I have Pepperidge Farm's crunchy grains bread. But I change it every day. I always have a bag on me and a bag of nuts for the squirrels. I know it's weird, but I feel like an outlaw carrying this stuff around."

We head to a supermarket on Eighty-ninth Street. Sally buys enough birdseed to fill two plastic shopping bags. I offer to carry one for her. She says no, she's used to it and likes to walk balancing equal weights. Her back is bent, her shoulders stooped, and the bags dangle just inches above the ground, but she moves surprisingly quickly. Anna and I can barely keep up with her. She won't slow down until all the birds are fed.

A block away, Sally cuts open a ten-pound bag with her apartment key and dumps it beside a fire hydrant. The seeds splash all over the curb and settle into thick piles. It's the avian equivalent of an all-points bulletin. Dozens of birds swoop in from blocks away, like people chasing after loose dollars blowing in the wind.

Sally doesn't stick around to watch the birds feast on her munificence. Instead, she hastily disappears back into the crowd. Her satisfaction seems to come from knowing that the birds have been fed. By comparison, Anna takes her time and tries to bond with each and every bird.

Sally decides to return to the supermarket for more seed. "I need ten pounds more. C'mon!" she barks. Waiting outside the store, Anna sees two sparrows sparring over a pizza crust and points them out to me. "Look at how hungry they are! Look! Look! I shouldn't feed them here right in front of the supermarket, but they look so hungry. Maybe I'll give them just a little something . . ."

On Ninety-sixth Street, Sally *bites* open a thick plastic bag of seed and spills it onto the sidewalk. Pigeons arrive out of nowhere. "They wait for me," she tells me. Sally is scheduled for a hospital procedure, and she's worried about the pigeons surviving while she's gone. Anna volunteers to staff Sally's feed route.

We walk to a small park where Sally catches her breath before we slog forward once again. Sally then buys yet more birdseed, this time at a supermarket on Second

Avenue. On the sidewalk, Anna spots a pigeon. "This little guy needs something to eat," she says, tossing him bread crumbs. More pigeons appear. Sally emerges with more bags of feed. "Okay," she says. "Let's march on!"

The expedition ends at a neighborhood park, where Anna feeds the squirrels. Inevitably, conversation returns to pigeons and Anna's conviction that more and more of them are disappearing. "One day there will be just one left, and we'll idolize it because it's the last one," Anna says. "I believe it's a strong possibility. Oh, God. How awful. And once they're done with the pigeons, they'll pick on the starlings. And when they're gone, they'll pick on the sparrows."

While Sally and Anna walk the streets of New York like pigeon pied pipers, another community of similarly obsessed pigeon lovers network for their favorite bird in the digital ether.

The plea for help was gut-wrenching. A flurry of increasingly desperate e-mails on the New York City "Pigeon People" listserv reported seeing a pigeon hanging upside down from a tree branch, five stories off the ground in a nearly inaccessible courtyard of an apartment complex. The pigeon's feet were tangled in a piece of string, and now that piece of string was tangled in a tree branch. The bird could be seen thrashing about, clearly unable to right itself, let alone break loose. Night was falling, and a fierce winter storm was fast approaching.

The virtual community sprang into action with their keyboards, but no one could think of a way to rescue the struggling pigeon. The Fire Department doesn't rescue birds, and a ladder truck couldn't access the courtyard regardless; a climber willing to scale the tree couldn't be located; and a helicopter would generate too much wind and cost too much. Could someone harpoon the tree from an apartment window and shuffle across the wire to retrieve the bird? Somebody suggested alerting the media, but who's going to write about a city pigeon trapped in a tree? A puppy, maybe. But a pigeon?

The snowstorm arrived and blanketed the city. The dangling bird swayed in the wind. The pigeon advocates were at a complete loss. Successive e-mails were filled with panic and dread. The exhausted bird's movements slowed to minute twitches. By morning it was covered in snow and ice, dead. The small group of New York pigeon lovers was devastated.

A year earlier, a red-tailed hawk by the name of Pale Male made international news when the owners of a posh Fifth Avenue apartment building attempted to relocate his nest overlooking Central Park. Thousands of people picketed the building and wrote letters of protest to media outlets around the city, keeping up a constant vigil.

The high-voltage scrutiny of being front-page news took its toll (it was a slow news week), and the building's management finally caved in. Pale Male's eviction was rescinded. To this day, hundreds of people continue to visit the site, not to protest but to peer up at the raptor's nest with telescopes and binoculars. Meanwhile, landlords and residents spend tens of millions of dollars to evict pigeons from well-established perches all across the city.

Most birds in the United States are protected by a series of federal laws and international treaties. The federal Migratory Bird Treaty Act of 1918, for instance, has been expanded to cover non-migratory birds, and now protects more than eight hundred wild species. Even the devious, egg-stealing blue jay is federally protected. Then there's the federal Endangered Species Act, which gives additional protection to birds such as bald eagles, condors, piping plovers, and the infamous spotted owl. Many of these birds and their habitats are additionally protected by the multimillion-dollar efforts of nonprofit avian charities such as the American Bird Conservancy and the National Audubon Society. (*Most* birds are popular. There are forty-six million bird-watchers in the United States alone.)

So where does the pigeon fit into these public and private avian safety nets? It doesn't. The rock dove is one of a small handful of commoners, such as starlings and sparrows, that can't gain entry to the exclusive club of desirable birds, leaving them without any legal protections. Local animal cruelty laws occasionally address pigeons, but more often than not, the birds are exempted from protection because of their status as nuisance animals. The Environmental Protection Agency terms the rock dove a pest, and Wildlife Services, a branch of the United States Department of Agriculture, actively participates in pigeon control operations in urban and agricultural areas (pigeons like to feast on cattle feed). The department averages about seventy-five thousand pigeon kills a year, often with the aid of Avitrol. The city of Chicago recently declared the keeping of pigeons *illegal*, regardless of whether they are bred for racing or beauty.

Why the discrimination? It's a matter of how you parse the words "wild" and "native." The rock dove is not, strictly speaking, wild. Having returned to an untamed state from domestication, the birds are now technically feral, and thus unprotected. Having sailed here with settlers (albeit hundreds of years ago and with no say in the matter) the rock dove can't be labeled a native species, unlike its cousin the passenger pigeon. Instead, it carries the stigma of being an introduced species. Unlike cardinals, blue jays, and robins, pigeons are designated an invasive species, much like the archenemy of any gardener—the dandelion. And how do we rid ourselves of dandelions and other hated weeds? We poison them. But unlike dandelions, pigeons are not actually displacing anything. Their only real crime is annoying another predominantly non-native species—Americans —by crapping all over the place. In fact, no country claims the rock dove as a native son, nor does any country specifically protect the bird.

Even devoted rock dove enthusiasts, such as pigeon racers and fancy pigeon breeders, look down on the city pigeon as a trash bird that gives their thoroughbreds and genetic beauties a bad name. And bird-watchers? They view any artificially introduced species as unnatural and therefore undesirable. You won't find many birders donning binoculars for pigeons.

That's not to say the street pigeon is without its fans and supporters. The Internet is filled with global discussion groups about rescuing injured pigeons. The members compare notes on antibiotics, broken wings, flushing out poisons, and anti-pigeon zoning ordinances. They share electronic photos of recovering birds, pray together for the dying ones, and bemoan the bias against what they consider a beautiful and majestic bird. It's a tight community in which members post multiple daily messages from places as far-flung as Europe, the Middle East, and California.

In addition to rehabbing pigeons, members also return lost racing pigeons to their owners by decoding racing bands. To maintain good public relations, racing organizations often thank these listservs for their help. But sadly, it's mostly window dressing. Unbeknownst to many of these bleeding hearts, oftentimes pigeon racers don't want their wayward birds returned. A homer that can't make it home has no value. Although the birds are shipped back to their owners with the best of intentions, their necks are often snapped upon arrival.

New York City is big enough to have its own pro-pigeon listserv, an underground network of kindhearted and somewhat reclusive individuals who view pigeons as sweet, lovable birds that animate the cityscape. They see themselves as the birds' caretaker, an underdog's buffer against the barbarian hordes armed with poisons, nets, and a vitriolic hatred.

They spot injured pigeons, frequently taking them home to their small apartments, where they spend countless hours and hundreds of dollars rehabbing them. A typical listerv posting looks something like this: "I spotted a pigeon with a hurt wing on 42nd Street and 9th Ave.—on the southwest corner—huddled up near the door of the Dunkin' Donuts . . . I wasn't able to catch it because there was too much traffic. Can someone check up on him? He's obviously in need of our help."

At about the same time the upside-down pigeon was slowly dying of exposure, a somewhat senile man by the name of Willie was in danger of eviction from his Queens apartment, along with his hundred pigeon friends. The Pigeon People listserv quickly swung into action. They tapped into the pigeon-loving virtual community, locating homes across the nation for the pigeons and collecting enough money to buy shipping crates. One member even accompanied Willie to housing court and discussed the situation with his assigned social worker.

But after days of tedious coordination, Willie changed his mind and wouldn't let his animal friends be relocated to safe homes. Instead, he locked himself in his dilapidated apartment and wouldn't return phone calls or open the door. Willie was evicted, and after years of cozy domestication, the pigeons were let loose to fend for themselves. Most surely died.

You could say that the Sallys, Annas, and listserv communities are the soup kitchens, medical clinics, and civil rights activists of the New York City pigeon movement, which lies just beneath the surface of the city's cultural consciousness. But dig a little deeper and you'll find a third and more radical movement—one that believes in other means to protect the lives of pigeons. They're a Weather Underground of sorts, fed up with writing editorials and helping one pigeon at a time. They've grown disenchanted with conventional means for safeguarding the lives of city pigeons, although they always remain within the boundaries of the law. While they strategize on how to topple the systemic persecution of pigeons, they also concentrate on what they see as the bird's greatest immediate threat: pigeon poachers.

Eduardo, a middle-aged New York City street vendor of knockoff watches and baseball hats, tells me how he befriended a young pigeon, named him Jimmy, and took him home to his basement apartment. Jimmy would eat out of Eduardo's hand but preferred to peck partially chewed crackers out of the soft-spoken vendor's mouth.

Every morning Eduardo would let Jimmy loose, and every afternoon the bird would be waiting for him when he got home. One day Eduardo, who sets up his table in the predawn hours, saw men exit a white van and toss birdseed at the pigeons. Moments later, the men threw a net over the birds, tossed them in the back of the van, and drove down the avenue.

Eduardo's eyes tear up as he finishes his story: That afternoon he walked home to an empty apartment. His beloved Jimmy was gone. "I know it was those evil men. They took Jimmy. They stole my little Jimmy." More likely than not, Jimmy ended up as a live target at a pigeon shoot in rural Pennsylvania. That is, if he survived the trip.

As if life weren't hard enough for a city pigeon, these survivors of inhumane traps and hungry predators must also contend with the profit-driven world of netters. In principle, netting is illegal. Feral pigeons are the property of the state and fall under the domain of the Department of Environmental Protection. According to state statutes, wild birds cannot be trapped without written permission, nor sold across state lines as shotgun fodder for gun clubs. But once again, the bird's feral status confuses the issue: Are pigeons truly wild? Even if pigeons didn't fall through the cracks, it's hard to imagine the state enforcing the law to protect them anyway.

The netters have free rein as long as they keep a low profile. They work under the cloak of near-darkness out of nondescript vans, often with the tacit approval of landlords sick of cleaning up after "winged cockroaches." But a tiny fringe group of anonymous spies is diligently working to punch a dent into the quasi-illegal trade. They call themselves Bird Operations Busted, or B.O.B.

It is a secretive organization run by a middle-aged Walter Mitty who fancies himself the 007 of the pigeon world. To protect his true identity, he also calls himself "Bob" He won't tell you how many "agents" belong to B.O.B. or their names. In fact, no member of B.O.B. knows anything about the other members of B.O.B., except, of course, Bob. They are assigned code names such as Space Bird, Native Bird, and Street Bird. (I suspect the latter is Eduardo.)

Bob tells me that these seemingly paranoiac precautions are for the safety of the organization's secret agents. "The netters are not happy with us," he explains. "They really hate us, because we spoil their profit margins."

"We are putting ourselves in jeopardy. I've had death threats. Not just one but many. They want my head. We use code names so that if information falls into the wrong hands, no one person can compromise other members."

Agents stake out their neighborhoods and report any suspicious pigeon activity. They are armed with disposable cameras and a blank form for recording license numbers, makes of vehicles, number of netters, time, location, and the number of captured birds. "Rain, sleet, snow—it doesn't matter. We are out there every day, keeping an eye on things, ready to ring the alarm bells," Bob tells me. "We are foot soldiers, the hard-core element of the pigeon movement. We have become a central pivot point. Actions get taken, things get done."

According to Bob, several notorious netting locations are monitored by video cameras located in members' apartments. He says he has over seven terabytes worth of video and other covert information divvied up and hidden among an undisclosed number of servers in undisclosed locations around the city. "We prefer not to discuss those matters," he informs me. "We don't want to alarm the authorities." He does, however, keep in touch with a cadre of animal-friendly journalists. "I can get something on television or published in a newspaper on a moment's notice if necessary."

The information is meticulously collected and re-corded in hopes that the netters will one day be prose-cuted. The group has at least one *pro bono* lawyer working on its behalf. But as one of their lawyers told me, it's an uphill battle. State law prohibits the trapping, netting, or snaring only of *wild* birds. Meanwhile, Bob and the rest of the agents continue spying on the netters, letting them know they're being watched. So far, only one pigeon poacher has been dragged into court, and that was for as-saulting one of Bob's agents and stealing his camera. (Bob says the man pled guilty to stealing the camera, but he continues to poach pigeons.)

And just who is this enigmatic Man from B.O.B.? I meet with him one spring afternoon on an Upper West Side street corner he has selected, not long after I inter-viewed Eduardo. As I wait, I have a sneaky suspicion I'm being watched. (Later, Bob would reveal to me that I was under video surveillance for much of the day.) A man dressed in black jeans, a black leather coat, and shaded bifocals approaches me. We start walking west. After a block, Bob glances around and then visibly relaxes.

Bob won't tell me his real name or where his for-eign accent is from. When he orders french fries at lunch and dips them in mayonnaise, I suspect he is Belgian. But then Bob lets drop between bites that he spent much of his childhood on a Caribbean island that was a former European colony. Which makes him . . . Dutch? A camera flash goes off at a nearby table, and Bob eyes the room suspiciously before continuing our conversation. Does he suspect I brought the heat?

He tells me that he had an "impressive and very successful career" in electrical engineering, broadcast engineering, theatrical lighting, and computer programming. He says Ray Dolby, the inventor of the eponymous noise reduction system, knows him by name, and that the inventor of streaming digital audio is personally indebted to him, or at least should be. "I was on the Internet in the mid-eighties," he says, "back when we called it 'phone phreaking.'" Disgusted by the corporate world, he began to focus his energies on helping animals.

Bob says he works 24/7 for his group, setting up video cameras around the city, collecting data, backing it up, and carefully feeding pigeons. "I have certain pigeons I keep an eye on," he confides, pulling a plastic sandwich bag partially filled with birdseed from his jacket pocket. He stealthily sprinkles a small amount behind a park bench.

Bob has a soft spot for all animals and has turned his apartment into a sanctuary for dying cats and wounded birds. He has a network of veterinarians who help him at cost or for free. "The cats are all old and abandoned by their owners. They are all terminal cases. It's just a matter of time. We give them fluids, pills, and wipe their butts because they are too old to keep themselves groomed. It's always an ending road, but we try to do it in a way that's as comfortable as possible for the kitty."

He's sickened by animal abuse and provides me with reams of data suggesting that cruelty to animals inevitably leads to violence against humans. The people who net pigeons, he explains, are motivated by the desire to abuse animals and are likely to be child and wife abusers as well—animals are merely a first step. Numerous studies have shown that societies that mistreat their animals are often violent societies overall.

Bob says he will one day establish a large animal asylum somewhere in the world to which he can devote all his energies. "I am not bound by any country, and I don't have to live by their corporate rules," he says. "There is animal abuse everywhere in the world."

A lifelong pigeon fan, Bob learned about netting by accident. Early one morning he saw some men netting birds outside his apartment. Instead of accosting them, he befriended them to learn more. What he heard horrified him. The poachers lure pigeons with seed, throw a big net over them, and then toss them in a truck. They can collect as many as a thousand birds in a single morning and sell them to restaurants and shooting clubs for a few bucks apiece.

Like Guy Merchant and Dave Roth, Bob was surprised to learn that no one in the city was doing anything about this nefarious pigeon trade. That was when he sprang into action. "It's a war being fought live every morning," he says.

Bob views education as an integral part of his job. He's familiar with many of the city's compulsive pigeon feeders and tries to tutor them on proper pigeon care and safety measures. First, he encourages feeders to lure the birds away from popular netting areas. It's best to feed away from the curb, where the birds are easy prey for

161

drive-by poachers, and even better to feed on rooftops. Feeders should also clean up after the birds. "Feeding and cleaning should go hand in hand," Bob says. He claims to spend several hours a day sweeping and scrubbing his own pigeon feeding areas.

Then there's the matter of feed. Pigeons given bread made from processed white flour tend to poo rock-hard droppings that can be so difficult to remove they practically require sandblasting. It is these concrete-like turds that give pigeons an even worse reputation, Bob says. He recommends feeding pigeons birdseed because it contains plenty of fiber. The resulting craps are bigger and perhaps more frequent, but they wash away easily in the rain, he explains.

"It's pitiful, but there are large populations of pigeons in this city who don't even know what birdseed is," Bob tells me. "All they know are bagels and pizza crusts. I've even seen two hawks fighting over a jelly doughnut." In Bob's world, it's the humans who are the slobs and the pigeons that generously clean up after us. "The pigeons are the day cleaning crew, and the rats are the night cleaning crew. Without them, we'd die in our own filth."

We walk to Verdi Square, a park popular with pigeons. Once there, Bob informs me that, "as of right now, there are four B.O.B. cameras recording us." One of his projects is training this park's pigeons to stay out of harm's way: "We can train these birds. We have probably trained one million already."

According to Bob, "We're on this planet because of the pigeons. They were here before us." Asked to clarify, he adds, "Seventy percent of us can thank these birds that our family line has continued. They have provided us with nourishment and carried our important messages."

Bob's vision is of pigeons and people living in complete and humane harmony all across the country. His future plans are to set up underground cells in Boston and Miami.

But Bob has more immediate pressing issues. "We have a problem, and it's very dangerous," he confides, voice lowered. A compulsive feeder on the Upper East Side is attracting thousands of pigeons, as well as the ire of his neighbors. Worse still, he's feeding them white bread and in a high-traffic area.

"He's not helping the birds. He's only creating a public nuisance and pissing people off. It's people like him that are ruining the bird's reputation. And that leads to poisonings. It's just this kind of downward spiral that B.O.B. is trying to reverse."

Abruptly, Bob informs me that the interview is over; pigeons are waiting. Mouthing goodbye, he quickly glides backward away from me. He trips over a fire hydrant. I avert my eyes out of embarrassment and look up seconds later. Bob is gone.

As elusive as Bob is, interviewing him was a relative cinch compared to gaining entry into the world of America's most infamous pigeon lover: Mike Tyson. As I struggled to push my way in, I found a world populated with all-night carousers, pathetic hangers-on, and, of course, pigeons.

9

Mike and Me

I've been doing this my whole life, longer than anything I've ever participated in besides breathing . . . It's like one of those boyhood diseases that you can't get out of your blood . . . I know people think I'm crazy because I'm a black, young, rich millionaire and I'm here flying pigeons, but this is what I've done all my life. I'm gonna die doing this.

—Mike Tyson speaking on ABC's
Jimmy Kimmel Live

COULD THERE BE A MORE CLASSIC DICHOTOMY, A MORE UN-usual pairing, than Iron Mike Tyson, former heavyweight champion of the world, and his gentle birds? And yet anyone who knows him knows that pigeons are far more important to him than boxing.

Tyson's rags-to-riches-to-rags story is legendary. Born into poverty to a broken home, Tyson grew up on the streets of Brownsville, Brooklyn, forty years before gentrification hit the borough's more fortunate neighborhoods. Some describe his existence then to that of a feral cat, rummaging for food and sleeping in abandoned buildings.

The one thing that kept him occasionally in check was his love of pigeons. Wildlife is hard to come by in Brooklyn. But there are always pigeons. For an awkward boy with a lisp, pigeons were easy companions. Tyson spent countless hours on rooftops squinting into the sky, watching his pigeons soar higher and higher. These birds knew freedom, and just observing them gave him a measure of calm and hope. Caring for them—feeding them, holding them in his outsize hands—gave him a measure of empathy and a routine.

It's said that Tyson's discovery of his unnerving ability to beat the crap out of someone involved pigeons. An older neighborhood bully grabbed one of Tyson's pigeons and twisted its neck until its head popped off. Tapping in to a manic anger that would later serve him well —and badly—the ten-year-old Tyson beat up the bully, which earned him a tough reputation in the neighborhood and may have led to his acceptance in gangs. It didn't take long before Tyson was engaging in muggings, robberies, and burglaries. At twelve, he was caught purse snatching and sent upstate to Tryon School for Boys.

By a stroke of luck, Tyson was introduced to legendary boxing trainer Cus D'Amato. Recognizing the boy's talent and looking for one last athlete to mentor into greatness, the elderly D'Amato agreed to take on Tyson. In time, the trainer harnessed Tyson's unfocused anger and channeled it into a rigorous schedule. D'Amato believed in Tyson and even legally adopted him.

D'Amato saw Tyson rise up through the amateur ranks, but he died one year before the twenty-year-old would be declared the youngest heavyweight champion in history. Tyson would have three more good years of pummeling opponents with insanely punishing knockout blows that earned him tens of millions of dollars. But it wouldn't take long for the troubled kid from Brownsville to get into trouble again. With D'Amato out of the picture, a rudderless Tyson publicly self-destructed over a period of years.

Tyson can probably count on one hand or less the number of people who have his best interests in mind. Ever since the death of D'Amato, predators have swarmed around the champ like bees to honey. By his early twenties, he was worth upward of $100 million and attracting a large entourage of parasites. He consistently trusted the wrong people: For a time, he even considered promoter Don King a close friend.

Which brings us back to Tyson's obsessive hobby. After all the abandonment and exploitation, guess whom Tyson turns to for unconditional love? Unlike his parents, ex-wife, girlfriends, so-called friends, fans, and promoters, his pigeons have never clung to him for the perks of celebrity, never sued him for a piece of his fortune and never taken advantage of his naive thirst for connection. The former champ retreated back to his pigeons, staring up at the sky to watch them soar without worry.

Tyson's particular attraction is to high-flying endurance birds that can stay aloft for as long as sixteen hours. These pigeons, called tipplers and flights, fly in endless circles above their lofts before returning at day's end. Owners of these breeds usually play a game in which they try to attract other high-flying neighborhood birds to their lofts. As powerful as the birds' urge is to return to their own lofts, sometimes the urge to play and mate with another flock is even stronger. It's a friendly game, with the losing loft owner paying the winner a small fee—say a dollar a bird—to get his pigeons back. It's played out day after day, year after year, from rooftops all across New York City. Tyson grew up playing this game and occasionally plays it still. But he's usually content just watching his birds soar for hours in circles far above him.

I'm eager to interview Tyson, but his erratic behavior makes him hard to pin down. He's burned so many bridges that, unlike most celebrities, he has no real management team, no one to take his calls and schedule interviews. I contact numerous national boxing writers but leave empty-handed and forewarned. "He's psychotic," one writer declares emphatically. "He's the most elusive interview in modern sports," another warns. Even a biographer of Tyson has few suggestions.

Finally, someone suggests I call Shelly Finkel, Tyson's sometime manager. Finkel's assistant insists I put my interview request in an e-mail that would then be faxed to Tyson. "There's no guarantee he will receive the fax or respond to it," she cautions, adding, "I wouldn't get your hopes up." I call back a few weeks later, as instructed.

"Did Mr. Tyson receive the fax?" I ask.

"Maybe."

"May I speak with Mr. Finkel?"

"Mr. Finkel is busy right now."

"When's a good time to call back?"

"Never."

Two part-time boxing writers who work for boxing Web sites prove more helpful. Mississippi-based Brad Cooney from Boxingtalk.com suggests I call Tyson's former trainer Freddie Roach. "He's one of the most decent guys in the business, and he's a good friend. Just use my name."

I call Roach at his gym in Los Angeles. He trained Tyson for his fights against Lennox Lewis and Danny Williams. I expect a cranky old man, like the trainer in *Rocky*, to give me the brush-off. Instead, I find myself chatting amicably with a youngish man who suffers from Parkinson's and occasionally slurs his words.

"Yeah, Mike loves his birds. He's like a little kid around them. He just totally lights up, totally relaxes. Outside of boxing, pigeons are definitely his passion. He's up at four A.M. working with them . . . It's kind of funny, I didn't know anything about pigeons until Mike introduced me to his. He just might be willing to talk with you about them."

"Do you know how I might contact Tyson?" I ask.

"I had a number for him, but it was disconnected . . . Basically, Mike contacts me when he needs me, and I have to sit around and wait for his call. He's not much for staying in touch. And I'm his trainer."

A week later, I receive a tip: Tyson is training in Vero Beach, Florida, with former champ Buddy McGirt. The local papers jump on the boxer's sordid past and describe his registration as a sex offender with the local police department. McGirt's gym is unlisted. I locate a number and call the gym, but the phone is never answered. I later learn that Tyson left McGirt to travel in Italy as a paid celebrity attendant at the San Remo music festival, much to the consternation of the Italian press, who question why a convicted rapist is being paid to wander around the event.

A few days later, I receive another tip: Tyson is back with Freddie Roach. "Yeah, he's back with us," says Justin Fortune, Freddie's friendly assistant trainer. "I'll be heading out to Phoenix to meet with him in a week. I'll ask him about the interview. He really loves pigeons, and I bet he'd be willing to talk with you about them. No worries."

Three days later, I hear that Tyson is training in Australia with former champ Jeff Fenech. Justin says the rumors are wrong and that Tyson is back in Phoenix, but Freddie's too busy training other prizefighters to take Tyson on right now. Roach's current star, featherweight champ Manny Pacquiao, is due to fight Erik Morales in Las Vegas in two weeks. Justin expects to meet Tyson for dinner after the fight. "Give me a call then, and we'll see what we can do for you," Justin offers. "He's always excited to talk about his birds."

Pacquiao narrowly loses the fight. I suspect morale is low in Freddie's camp but call Justin at one A.M., as scheduled. "I'm just getting dressed to have dinner with you-know-who," Justin says. "Mind calling me in an hour or two, and we'll see about that interview?"

I call Justin at three A.M. No answer. I leave several messages, but still no Justin. I reach him a few days later. He says he ended up driving Pacquiao to the hospital for stitches and missed dinner with Tyson altogether. "I'm sorry I'm not being much help. But I do think he'll talk to you. Pigeons *are* his passion."

The writer Brad Cooney e-mails me. "Remember, I said an interview with Tyson is possible, but not probable," he cautions. Another Internet boxing writer, Michael Doss of Houston, suggests I contact his boss, John Raygoza of 15rounds.com. "He gave Tyson some pigeons, and now they're sort of friends," Doss offers. "They live near each other in Phoenix. He should be able to hook you up."

Raygoza doesn't respond to my e-mails for three weeks. Then again, I'm told he's a big shot at a large computer company, and 15rounds.com is more of a hobby for him. He has a cell phone number, but Michael says he doesn't like using it because the minutes cost so much. . . .

Another week passes before Michael e-mails me with big news: Tyson *is* training with Jeff Fenech, but in downtown Phoenix at a place called the Central Boxing Club. "Call John again. He's a good friend with the gym owner. I think we are close, my friend!"

I call Raygoza, and he tells me his pigeon story involving Tyson. "I bought him two high-flying tipplers. I was new in town, and I wanted to meet him. I heard he liked pigeons, so I figured I'd buy him a pair. Trouble was, I didn't know anything about pigeons. I didn't even know there were so many kinds of them. I just Googled 'pigeon breeders and Phoenix' and e-mailed a bunch of people. Only one breeder responded to my e-mail. He asked me what kind of pigeons I wanted, and I said I didn't really know. Somehow he knew—I don't know how—that I was buying birds for Tyson. He said Tyson likes tipplers, so I bought two of them. A boy and a girl."

The breeder educated Raygoza about the birds. "It was Pigeons 101. He gave me just enough info to get me in Tyson's front door."

The next day Raygoza rushed to the gym to present the birds. Tyson wasn't there. Being Tyson, he had unexpectedly left town and wouldn't be returning for a month. Raygoza left the gym "feeling like shit" and with two strange birds in tow.

"I didn't know what to do with the birds. I didn't even really like them. And now I was stuck with them for a month or more. I went to a pet store and got some bird food and took them back home. After fifteen days, I was starting to lose hope, so I just let them go and watched them fly away. I thought, Good riddance. But the next morning, they were right back on my balcony. That's when I fell in love. That's when I learned to respect them. I started letting them out every day. I learned that if I clapped, they flew higher and higher. One day I even found eggs in the cage. But I didn't know what to do with them."

Tyson returned at last. "He was excited when he saw the birds. He said, 'You're my new friend. Come to my house. Let's go fly the pigeons.' We went right to his house, and he showed me a little stable of pigeons in his backyard. He had all kinds of pigeons, but they all look the same to me. He said he didn't like his show pigeons so much because he thinks they're lazy. He likes the high fliers because they like to work out and exercise. They remind him of himself."

Raygoza's moment of basking in the champ's sunshine came to an abrupt end when he mentioned he was a boxing writer and would like to interview him. "The music stopped immediately. You could see he was pissed off. The smile was gone. He looked at me and said, 'You're a sportswriter? I can't believe I let a writer in my house. You can leave now.' We had been watching old boxing videos of famous fights. He turns off the TV right away and waits for me to leave.

"Tyson has a reputation. Everybody knows he's temperamental. I figured my visit would turn south at some point anyway. But just as I'm opening my car door, he comes out and asks where I got the birds. I tell him where and give him directions. Then he jumps in his Rolls-Royce and speeds off."

Raygoza isn't sure where the peripatetic Tyson now lives. He had been living with a Brazilian girlfriend in north Phoenix. He's now rumored to live somewhere in

Scottsdale. Tyson is known for changing his address often. We agree that my best opportunity to meet Tyson is to just show up at the gym. Raygoza says he will smooth the way with the gym manager, a young African-American by the name of Harwood.

I call the breeder who sold Raygoza the pigeons. He's a high school student named Dean Lazic who emigrated from Serbia with his family in the late 1990s. Dean has since sold many birds to Tyson and visited his loft. "He's a good breeder," Dean says. "He's very gentle with his birds. He really knows his stuff. He keeps his loft clean and his birds healthy. It's his number one thing." Dean says that Tyson told him about growing up with birds in Brooklyn. "He said he didn't have a lot of money back then and would clean a guy's pigeon coop for a pair of pigeons."

Dean tells me that Tyson is a member of the Arizona Pigeon Club and eagerly attends most local pigeon shows, often buying winning birds to breed into his flock. "He has some of the prettiest birds I've seen in Arizona. He has some with black lace, which is a very rare coloring. But he also breeds for endurance." Tyson's continuing passion for pigeons, I realize, is easy to understand. "With pigeons, it's always something new," Dean continues. "When you're breeding, there are always new babies, new colors, new challenges."

The morning after I arrive in Phoenix, I get a hurried e-mail from Michael Doss: "I hope you haven't left for Arizona yet. I just got word that Tyson is leaving for the East Coast to announce his upcoming fight. I told you Tyson was unpredictable! Lol!" I race to the gym in central Phoenix and introduce myself to Harwood. I tell him I'm friends with Raygoza. But Harwood is tight-lipped. "Mike ain't here," he says.

Tyson's press conference is scheduled for Monday in Washington, D.C., where the fight will take place in a few months. The fight is designed to boost the soon-to-be-thirty-nine-year-old's confidence. Many in the press are already calling Tyson washed up. But he's expected to knock out Irish journeyman Kevin McBride in two rounds, maximum. All my contacts generally agree that Tyson will be back at the gym to train the next day, or Wednesday at the latest.

Saturday night, Raygoza invites me to grab a beer and watch a televised fight with Harwood. I suspect that after a few friendly beers at a sports bar, Harwood will help me meet Tyson. I follow Raygoza's directions to the bar and unexpectedly find myself in a distant and seedy section of Phoenix filled with pawnshops, used car dealer-ships, and derelicts wandering around aimlessly. I pull into a parking lot that matches the address. The cozy sports bar I had imagined turns out to be a strip club humming with Friday-night testosterone. I'm surprised to find Harwood minding the entrance. "What are you doing here?" he shouts over the pulsating music. I'm dumbfounded: Harwood is the *bouncer* and doesn't even know why I am there. I ask him if Raygoza is around, and he brusquely points to a far corner before patting me down for weapons.

"I hope meeting here is all right," Raygoza says. "I certainly didn't want you to regret your trip." After several rounds of drinks, he tells me Tyson's favorite strip club isn't far away and that we can go there as well.

Our table backs up on a row of red-upholstered benches against the wall. A knuckle presses against the back of my chair and into my shoulder. A mane of blond hair sweeps across my face. Not two feet behind me, a man is getting a lap dance. The dancer is using my chair to steady herself as she gyrates her ass in the patron's face.

Raygoza flirts with his favorite dancer. I'm wondering how this will improve my chances of meeting Tyson next week. I find myself in conversation with a Mexican waitress who calls herself Trixie. We both have five-month-old daughters at home and compare notes. Is her daughter sleeping through the night? Which diapers do I use? We both bemoan how quickly they grow up, how quickly time marches on. We're interrupted when the lap dancer behind me briefly looses her balance. Her breasts knock into the back of my head.

Raygoza assures me that Harwood will get me in the gym. "No problem," he says with absolute confidence and then orders a lap dance. I excuse myself and head for the taco truck across the street.

At night's end, Raygoza gives me a proper introduction to Harwood. "I'd appreciate it if you'd take care of my friend. He's here to talk to Tyson about pigeons." Harwood remains noncommittal, his muscular arms crossed. "Yeah, I know," he says. I leave as soon as is politely possible.

On Sunday, I learn that Tyson's press conference has been delayed until Tuesday. When the day comes, he arrives with three of his children and sums up the upcoming fight. "I just hope the people of Washington, D.C., are prepared to handle this. It's going to be a train wreck." A reporter asks Tyson how much longer he will continue to fight, given that he is still $30 million in debt. "Long enough to take care of my children—a long time," Tyson responds. Raygoza assures me that Tyson is expected back at the gym on Wednesday.

When Wednesday arrives, I head to the gym. Tyson is supposed to show up at one P.M. and work out for two hours, as usual. I arrive at noon and sit on the curb. A street pigeon hangs out beside me and pecks at a crust of bread. A local artist is perched on scaffolding above the front entrance, painting a mural of Tyson.

Harwood walks across the street carrying a bag of burritos and talking into his cell phone. He looks at me sternly, as if we've never met. "You got to understand, Mike needs to concentrate on his training. He doesn't need to be interrupted by *guys like you*. You're one of five hundred people hanging around here trying to get an interview with him."

I look around the empty parking lot. "I'm just waiting here on the sidewalk," I say. "If Tyson doesn't want to talk with me, fine. That's his right. But I'd just like a chance to ask him."

"Not on my sidewalk, you ain't."

His sidewalk? Sensing trouble, the pigeon at my feet flies away. "Do you expect Tyson at one P.M.?" I ask.

"Tyson ain't here, and as far as you're concerned, he's never coming back." Harwood storms off. Given his background as a bouncer, he's doing what he does best —protecting his client.

"Maybe you should write Tyson a letter," the muralist on the scaffolding lamely offers.

I walk across the street and call Raygoza. Harwood is writing down the license plate on my rental car and patrolling the sidewalk. Raygoza puts me on a conference call with his "good friend."

"You got to respect his position," Raygoza argues on my behalf. "He's flown all the way from the East Coast to meet Tyson. He's been waiting around for a week."

"I ain't respecting shit," Harwood counters.

"Just let him do his job. You're not a patrol officer."

"If he trespasses in my parking lot, I'll have him arrested," I can hear Harwood screaming across the street and a split second later on my cell phone.

"That's a *public* parking lot," Raygoza reminds Harwood.

"Well, I'll get a restraining order and a warrant for his arrest. And for you, too, if you come down here!"

Apparently, my trip to the strip club didn't advance my cause. The phone call ends in a stalemate. It's now approaching two P.M. Tyson is obviously not showing up.

Harwood cools off and walks across the street toward me. "You can save yourself a lot of time and leave now, because Mike's not in town." He sees my skepticism and then dials a number on his cell phone. He hands me the phone so I can talk with Tyson's right-hand man, a guy named Darryl.

"If you're a fan of Mike's, as I'm sure you are, you understand that he's training for the biggest fight of his career and needs to be in total isolation," says Darryl of the laughably mismatched upcoming fight. "You're just setting yourself up to get your feelings hurt by waiting around there. Mike won't have time to talk with you."

I hang up and ask Harwood, who won't tell me his own full name, for Darryl's last name. "Darryl," he says angrily. "Just Darryl."

On my way out of Phoenix, I call the writer Michael Doss. "Tyson's the most unpredictable man on the planet, but this is pathetic," he says. He offers to call Shelly Finkel himself to set up an interview; he says they're friendly. I'm put on another conference call. Michael asks to speak with Shelly, who's gone for the day. Michael asks how we can set up an interview with Tyson. He's told to send an e-mail that will be forwarded to Tyson, but the assistant isn't optimistic. "I wouldn't get your hopes up," she says.

Several weeks later, the boxing world is stunned when the unremarkable Kevin McBride actually knocks Tyson out. The former champ is photographed sitting in the corner against the ropes, looking depressed and washed out after his halfhearted effort. The poignant portrait is broadcast across the world. Tyson is clearly out of the fight business. He no longer has the stomach for it, he says.

He tells reporters after the fight that he just wants to go home and be with his pigeons.

Summer

10

Great Expectations

THE OLD-BIRD RACING SEASON BEGINS IN APRIL AND RUNS through early June. Orlando Martinez isn't racing his old birds this year because, loath as he is to admit it, they didn't do well last year. He's putting all his eggs in his young birds' basket: His sights are set on October's Main Event.

Another reason is money. The old-bird season stakes are traditionally very low, usually just a few hundred dollars per race. But young-bird races can be surprisingly lucrative. When young birds are born, their owners buy them special race bands, called futurities, which, for some races, can cost as much as $100 apiece.

Money aside, the young-bird races still brim with the bravado and excitement of the unknown. "Young birds are exciting because they've never raced before," Orlando says. "It's about hope. Everybody's got great expectations."

Orlando's bias for young-bird races doesn't mean he sits out the old-bird season completely. He's still a fixture at the races, and on a warm night in June, he's back at the Borough Park Homing Pigeon Club helping his friend Chester Szwaba—a pipe fitter in his mid-twenties—ship his old birds. Orlando used to race with Chester's father, who died a few years ago. Chester's grandfather also raced pigeons.

The birds from Borough Park and several other local clubs are packed sixteen to a crate and loaded onto a communal truck. They will be driven six hundred miles overnight to London, Ohio, five hundred air miles from Brooklyn. Billy Glynn, a slight, soft-spoken old man in a plaid fishing shirt and khakis, waits outside as the birds are loaded onto his truck.

"I'm the liberator," he says. "It's a big responsibility. I don't just drive a truck. There's a lot more to it. I know how much to feed them, and if the weather is good enough for them to be released. And they all have to be released at once. Not to put a medal on myself, but they can't get a lot of guys to do it. I've missed funerals, weddings, birthdays, even my grandson's high school graduation."

It's a tedious job, and Glynn says he's not sure why he does it. "I don't know. I enjoy driving. I guess that's why. Tonight I'll probably drive three hundred miles and then take a rest. An hour's all I need. Then I'll take it all the way down the turnpike. The roads are good at night. Before the race, I got to find a place where I can hook up a hose so I can feed them and give them water. Like I said, it's more than just driving a truck. It's a lot of responsibility."

The fifteen hundred birds on the truck are oddly tranquil. They walk about, clean themselves, and generally act as if being ripped from their nests, shoved into crates, and loaded onto a truck is old hat. In fact it is: These are the grizzled veterans of at least one prior racing season.

Inside the club, the air is filled with suspense. One question is on everyone's mind: Who will win? Orlando breaks the tension with a story about Chester's father, who used to cull losers from his loft and take them to friends who owned a restaurant in Chinatown.

"So one time he stops by, and they invite him sit and eat with them," Orlando says. "But he takes one look at the bird on his plate, and it still has the band around its leg. So Chester's dad's like, 'I can't eat him, that's my two-six-seven.'"

There's little of that joviality on display the next afternoon when Orlando stands in the bright sunshine on Chester's rooftop coop and waits for the old birds to fly home. The loft is eye level with the cars on the Brooklyn-Queens Expressway and so close to the noisy elevated roadway that Chester has named his coop the BQE Loft. It's infernally hot on the black tar roof, and there's not a lick of shade.

"The lead bird's not going down," Orlando shouts into his cell phone. "Listen. The lead bird's not going down. The winner isn't going down. He wants to win because he wants to come home. He's probably so tired and cramped, he can't get his landing gear down. But he doesn't care if he's in pain. He wants to come home." He hangs up, and the phone quickly rings again. "What? Charlie saw one three miles away? He's not sure it's a race bird? Okay. Check it out and let me know." The phone rings yet again. "Yes, Mamí. I love you." Orlando hangs up. "She wants to know I'm okay. She's the sweetest mother in the world." His mother seems to call every hour or so, but then again it's hard to tell: Orlando is in the habit of calling most females, pigeons and Omayra included, Mamí.

Orlando looks west. "This fucking tailwind is pushing them right home. If this were a short race, they'd be coming in like cannonballs." He estimates the birds will fly the five hundred miles in under eight hours.

The waiting is killing Chester. He walks around the roof and talks excitedly about the sport. "It's like a bug, a bug inside you that you can't get out. You got to be dedicated. I don't eat until my birds eat. I fed them a lot of carbs last night—" Chester pauses midsentence and points at a black dot fifty yards away. "There she is!" he shouts. "My bird! I knew it!"

Orlando grabs two hooples—tools resembling giant flyswatters that are used to coax birds back into the coop—and rushes toward the bird, which has now landed. "Come on, Mamí, come on," Orlando coos seductively. Chester approaches with a handful of raw Spanish peanuts. "It's like their steak or lobster," Orlando says. "A pigeon will do anything for a raw Spanish peanut."

After navigating five hundred miles home, the bird looks skinny and exhausted, as if she has lost some of her breast meat. Her mouth is open, gasping for water and air. But she's reluctant to enter the loft where Chester can grab her race band and time-stamp it with the clock. She sits on top of the coop staring wearily at the man with the giant flyswatters. Five precious minutes pass before she finally hits the landing board and enters the coop.

None of this dampens Chester's enthusiasm for the homing phenomenon. "She's an awesome pigeon. They get nervous, is all, just like people. And look. There's no mud on her feet. She didn't stop. She flew right through!"

Homing pigeons are also called carrier pigeons and messenger pigeons, and for this reason, people frequently confuse them with the similarly named passenger pigeon. But unlike passenger pigeons, homers don't live in the wild, and are particularly prized for their well-developed homing abilities. The instinct originated with the bird's need to forage for food and find its way back to its nest, much like the biblical white dove from Noah's Ark. Even today wild rock doves continue to nest in sea cliffs and forage for food deep inland.

This natural homing instinct has been enhanced by selective breeding. To begin with, the modern racing homer is actually a combination of eight different breeds of rock dove, including the English carrier pigeon. This hybrid is a sort of super-homing pigeon with a particularly aerodynamic and muscular body and an enhanced homing ability. The breed is further augmented when breeders carefully cull lesser birds and propagate only homers proven to be swift fliers and navigational wizards. This quest for a faster and smarter pigeon is relentless and has led to the creation of homers that can now fly distances of five to eight hundred miles (versus under a hundred miles in ancient times) at speeds greater than 60 mph. Gender has little bearing on athletic performance; male and female homers are equally strong fliers.

The white doves that you see released at weddings and other ceremonies are actually homers, sometimes even retired racers. They whoosh around dramatically in the sky for a few moments before they seemingly disappear like heavenly messengers. In actuality, the birds are simply orienting themselves before racing back to their home loft where they will recuperate before performing again. Other doves, such as the mourning dove, cannot home and would simply fly away upon release (making for an impractical business model). Ignorance of this fact has led to some unfortunate incidents. When the organizers of Jersey City's first memorial to 9/11 couldn't find any doves to release (they were reserved for other ceremonies), they went to a nearby poultry market and bought eighty white baby pigeons, or "squab." Not only had these youngsters never flown before, they weren't even homers. They were likely white kings, a breed of rock dove that is bred for its abundant breast meat, not its homing abilities. Once released, they shakily flew into spectators, nearby windows, and the New York harbor.

But how do these birds home? To solve this riddle, I contacted Charlie Wolcott, a professor of neurobiology and behavior at Cornell and a renowned pigeon navigation specialist. Wolcott has spent the better part of forty years attaching radio transmitters to pigeons and tailing them in a single-engine propeller plane. Like many naturalists, Wolcott specializes in the sort of natural esoterica that few of us would think to consider. His doctoral thesis was on spider hearing (they perceive sound with their legs), and he's currently working on the magnetic orientation of honeybees and the vocal communications of loons.

I was surprised to learn that he remains as perplexed by pigeon physiology as he was when he first looked into the matter in the early 1960s. "There are lots of theories and lots of information, but it doesn't all come together neatly," Charlie tells me. His frank attempts to answer my questions are frequently punctuated with a cheerful "We dunno!" or a playful "No reason, it's just our policy."

According to Charlie, the ability to navigate requires two skills. First, a bird needs to know where it is in relation to its home—after all, what good is a compass if you don't know where you are? Second, a bird needs to determine how to find its way back.

Since homers can find their way home from a place they've never been, it stands to reason that they must somehow figure out where they are. This feat alone is nothing short of astounding. Imagine being blindfolded and driven five hundred miles from your home. Would you be able to pinpoint your new location on a map? And keep in mind that some homers are raced from a thousand miles away.

Assuming you could orient yourself (say you've been driven to a distant but recognizable landmark such as the St. Louis Arch), now envision the shortest route home, and be prepared to revise your course en route. Also, you'll travel at the speed of a car in fifth gear and never stop to rest or refuel. Few of us have *any* of these capabilities. Even Magellan and the explorers of yore had to rely on sextants, compasses, and chance. But the rock dove has *all* of these capabilities, and in the modern homing pigeon they are highly refined.

Pigeons rely on a number of directional aides that are part of their biological makeup. First, it uses the sun's position to orient itself and find its loft. Pigeons also recognize that the sun rises in the east and sets in the west. And they have an internal clock and compass that help them judge their precise location in relation to the sun's movement.

A blindfolded pigeon can also find its loft, albeit with greater difficulty, which means that it must have at least one more navigational tool. The bird's so-called second compass senses the earth's magnetic field, which emanates from the planet in large, curved bands that are strongest at the poles and weakest at the equator. Charlie Wolcott's research leads him to believe that pigeons can measure the angle and strength of this magnetic field and position themselves accordingly. Then again, Charlie isn't entirely sure, either.

But he is sure that the magnetic field plays a role. He and his students placed magnetized coils around several birds' heads and drove them away from their home loft. When Charlie reversed the polarity of the coils, the birds flew in exactly the wrong direction—away from home. Charlie was also the first to discover minute amounts of magnetic iron ore (magnetite) in the birds' heads. "We found itsy-bitsy chunks of it in the neural cells of the upper beak . . . We're not really sure how that works, either, but it does seem to help them sense the magnetic field." Other animals, including migratory birds, sea turtles, and even lobsters, are believed to make similar use of the magnetic field.

A Belgian study has linked unusual race occurrences to serious disturbances in the earth's magnetic field caused by solar storms, sunspots, and solar eclipses. One such example is the lost birds of Pennsylvania mystery, when hundreds of homers lost their way. Two races were held on October 5, 1998: a 200-mile race from northern Virginia to Allentown, Pennsylvania, and a 150-mile race from western Pennsylvania to Philadelphia. Out of 2,500 birds, only 300 made it home that day. Typically, only 5 to 10 percent of the birds lose their way during a race. The missing birds were spotted in Ohio, New Jersey, and West Virginia before reorienting themselves and returning home days later.

British racing birds that have disappeared while crossing the English Channel have been known to resurface as far away as New York's Long Island Sound and even the South China Sea. This, however, has more to do with bad weather causing some birds to hitch rides on freighters and cruise ships.

An especially keen sense of hearing also helps pigeons navigate. They are able to hear infrasound as low as one tenth of a hertz. By comparison, we are unable to hear anything below twenty hertz, approximately the sound of the lowest organ pipe, which we feel more than we actually hear. Infrasound travels long distances, which leads researchers to speculate that pigeons are capable of hearing wind blow across the Rockies from two thousand miles away.

Visual and olfactory cues appear to help pigeons navigate the last few miles home. In one experiment, Charlie Wolcott placed frosted contact lenses on his pigeons, which hindered their normally excellent ultraviolet vision. The birds made it most of the way home but were then stymied. Evidently, pigeons, like humans, rely on landmarks to guide them. Similarly, Charlie anesthetized the birds' noses and found that this, too, hindered their ability to get home. Although he's not sure of the significance, Charlie has also learned that the birds are very sensitive to barometric pressure, and that their feet are receptive to minute vibrations.

"The more we study pigeon navigation, the more we see how little we understand it," Charlie finally offers. "It's one of the great mysteries of biology. Much of what we think we know is really just speculation. Sorry about that."

One thing everyone can agree on is that homers get better with practice, which is why fanciers such as Orlando are religious about their training regimes. It's not uncommon for pigeons to take off in the wrong direction and reorient themselves until they've corrected the deviation in midflight. The more familiar a bird is with the terrain, the more developed its internal map will be, and the quicker it will be to find its way home.

Regardless of why they do it, homers return home, and every racer has his own stories to tell. Orlando's favorite involves his bird Marty, who always placed well in competitions. One day she didn't return home from a three-hundred-mile race. Orlando assumed a hawk had eaten her. But two weeks later, he found Marty sitting on his door stoop with a broken wing.

She had walked home.

Orlando pulls up to a deserted parking lot beside an abandoned factory on Staten Island's northern shore. It's an ugly patch of weed-infested asphalt. Heat from the pavement distorts vision and bakes the skin. It's midsummer, and Orlando is training his young birds for the autumn races. The Main Event is still a good four months away, but Orlando couldn't be busier.

While some men spend a lifetime in search of a perfect trout stream or a flawless golf swing, Orlando has spent his free time driving around Staten Island searching for something this parking lot offers: a perfect trajectory to his pigeon loft.

Orlando climbs out of his battered blue pickup and reaches into the truck bed to inspect his precious cargo.

He grins broadly. Inside are several wooden crates filled with softly cooing homers. "We're exactly due west from my pigeon loft, ten-point-three air-miles," Orlando says, pointing across a hazy New York harbor to Brooklyn's skyline. Sandwiched somewhere in the jumbled mass is Orlando's town house with its rooftop coop, a place to which these young pigeons will spend a lifetime returning.

Orlando's racing clubs fly westerly races, and the homestretch of every race passes high above this abandoned parking lot. "When they reach this spot, the birds will be tired, hungry, and thirsty, and I don't want anything to make them deviate from going home," Orlando says. "I'm teaching them to fly a straight line. They won't even know they're doing it. They'll have done it too many times."

Orlando, who rarely sits still even for a meal, stops pacing and stands motionless. He raises his eyebrows emphatically. "This is why I always kick everybody's ass on race day. I guarantee you my birds will kick ass this year. I guarantee it. It'll be impossible for them not to." Another emphatic pause, followed by a look of frank sincerity. "Impossible."

Orlando takes the entire summer off to train his pigeons for the Main Event, although "vacation" can be a relative term for him. Ask Orlando what he does for a living, and you'll get more than one answer. Answer number one: "I clean pigeon coops. Mine." Answer number two: "I'm a freelance graphic artist. I like the way that sounds." Answer number three: "Telecommunications."

Work for Orlando is an occasional necessity that must be wedged into his yearly pigeon-racing schedule. "I race pigeons," he says. "That's what I do." Orlando insists he has turned down jobs paying in the high five figures because they interfered with caring for his pigeons. "I can get a job anytime I want," he says. "Not to sound arrogant, but I'm pretty much a borderline genius. One day on the job and I've mastered it . . . Finding work is not a problem."

Orlando dedicates a vast amount of time to his pigeons, especially during summer training. He wakes up before five A.M. so he can get in his first toss of the day before the morning rush hour, and he fits in two or three more training flights before sundown.

He places the crates on the cracked asphalt and waits. The birds rest quietly. They are orienting themselves, their brains like compass needles settling on a direction. When the birds begin to gently peck one another, it's called "music," and it means they're ready to fly. It's two P.M. and already the third training flight of the day.

Orlando opens a little mesh door on one of the crates and lets out five birds. Their wings flutter excitedly as they scamper out. Quickly airborne, they swoop and whoosh around frantically in pattern, flying left, and right, and then under a set of softly humming electrical wires. Orlando winces and shields his eyes, images of Kentucky Fried Pigeon filling his mind. The birds make it through the wires unharmed, regroup, and swing out toward Brooklyn and home. Orlando checks his watch and waits five minutes before releasing another set of pigeons. He wants each bird to learn to lead and not just follow the pack. After all, even a paper bag blowing in the wind might find its way home. Orlando wants his birds to *race* home.

Back at the rooftop loft in Brooklyn, Omayra sunbathes on a lounge chair, listens to salsa, and waits for the birds to return. Beside her rests a hoople and a bag of raw

Spanish peanuts. Orlando and Omayra telephone back and forth like teenagers, awaiting the birds. If it's not Omayra calling Orlando, it's his bird buddies trading gossip, or his mother. "Yes, Mamí," he says. "Yes, of course I love you."

Eleven minutes after the launch, Omayra calls with the good news: The first birds have arrived ten minutes faster than last week. In coming days, Orlando will release the birds at ever farther distances, from truck stops along the New Jersey and Pennsylvania turnpikes, some as far as 125 air miles from his home. But he will end each day with a drive across the Verrazano Bridge to this parking lot for yet another toss.

"You can't just race pigeons," Orlando reflects. "You might win a race, but it'll be by accident, probably because some other guy made a mistake. If I win a race, it's not luck. I'm training them four times a day. What's lucky about that?"

Orlando's right. Hard work *is* the name of the game. It's a mantra that I will hear again and again as I tour Europe in search of the sport's humble beginnings. It's in Europe that I will trace the Birdman of Brooklyn's passion to the doorstep of Sandringham House, Queen Elizabeth II's private estate in East Anglia. The world, I will soon learn, is densely populated with pigeon fanatics.

11

The Old Bird's Birds

KING GEORGE V REFERRED TO SANDRINGHAM HOUSE AS "the place I love better than anywhere." The sumptuous estate is situated on twenty-two thousand acres in East Anglia and surrounded by miles of forests and fens. It's easy to see why Elizabeth II's grandfather was so fond of it.

Queen Victoria purchased the land in 1862 as a gift for her son, Albert "Bertie" Edward, Prince of Wales. A carefree Bertie frolicked here with his wife and children during his interminable wait to ascend the throne as King Edward VII. The house is filled with photographs of the young family riding in horse-drawn sleighs and picnicking on the estate's manicured grounds.

One might think that the lure of the estate for Edward's son, George V, might have faded with the outbreak of World War I. The king recruited his gardeners, groomsmen, and gamekeepers to serve in the war by creating the Sandringham Company, which served under the 1/5th Norfolk Regiment. Not one year later, all the men of Sandringham—fathers, sons, and brothers—were annihilated during their very first engagement, the infamous Battle of Gallipoli. Last glimpsed charging into merciless enemy fire, the company disappeared without a trace. It is now believed the Turkish soldiers captured the men, summarily executed them, and tossed their bodies into unmarked graves.

Unlike Buckingham Palace and Windsor Castle, which are state property, Sandringham belongs to the royal family. Queen Elizabeth and Prince Philip are fond of the residence and hunting grounds. Philip enjoys riding around the estate in antique carriages and practicing his favorite sport, dressage. The royal family spends a month or two there each winter and several weeks each summer, at which time the estate's staff swells to nearly 250.

Despite Sandringham's rich history and surroundings, in his heart of hearts, Carlo Napolitano wishes he could pick it up and plop it down somewhere else. Carlo races pigeons—the queen's pigeons. And when it comes to pigeon racing, Sandringham is horribly situated. The estate is a mere stone's throw from a lamentable obstacle called the Wash, a shallow semicircular estuary about twenty-two miles across. It represents a fragile truce of sorts between humanity's agricultural ambitions and the land-hungry North Sea.

For hundreds of years, residents have battled the North Sea, whose briny swamplands once nearly reached Cambridge. Their persistence has been rewarded with tens of thousands of acres of rich mineral-laden soil. But it remains a constant struggle against a powerful foe—a series of rugged channels, dikes, and levies are all that keep these lowlands from being forcibly reclaimed by the sea.

The queen's birds race from the north, from as far away as Scotland and the northern Shetland Islands. While a pigeon will fly across water, it loathes it. The rock dove may nest on sea cliffs, but it always flies inland to forage for food. When faced with the choice, most pigeons will fly around a large body of water. Whether it's a five-hundred-mile race or a hundred-miler, the queen's pigeons are faced with the same decision at the tail end of every race: Should they take their chances and fly across the Wash, or should they play it safe and take the long way around it? They often choose the latter.

Given the unlikelihood of Sandringham's relocation, Carlo is forced to endure the ribbing from fellow racers at the local pub in nearby King's Lynn, none of whom, by the way, suffer a similar logistical fate. Handicapped or not, Carlo is a master racer and provides the queen with her fair share of wins. It's a good thing, because Her Majesty keeps score. "She's competitive," says Carlo. "She wants to know the results."

The queen's pigeons are descendants of a gift from Belgium's King Leopold to her great-grandfather King Edward VII. The birds were also of keen interest to both her grandfather King George V and her father, King George VI. Several photos on the estate show a young Elizabeth happily posing with her father in front of the family pigeon loft. Queen Victoria was also an admirer of pigeons, especially Jacobins, and kept a large loft of fancy breeds.

These days the royal family's interest in pigeons appears to be driven more by nostalgia. Queen Elizabeth II is far more passionate about her thoroughbred horses and her precious corgis. Nevertheless, she remains the honorary head of the Royal Pigeon Racing Association and a member of the local pigeon racing club, where Carlo competes in her name against local masons, mechanics, and blacksmiths.

Day-to-day management of the royal loft has always been left to professionals (Carlo is the fourth royal loft manager) who come from working-class backgrounds. The upper echelons of England's stratified social hierarchy politely refer to pigeon racing as a "cloth cap" sport. A third-generation barber and former amateur boxer who now distributes gaming machines to local pubs and seashore arcades as a day job, Carlo was a friend of the previous royal loft manager, though he has no idea how he was tapped for the job in the early 1990s. One moment he was racing against the queen (and beating her regularly, he likes to point out), and the next, he was living in a cozy rent-free home on the estate and caring for the queen's birds.

The otherwise unpaid job affords him other small luxuries, like traveling as the queen's representative to international races and conventions. "Some people think I'm bloody royalty. They even call me 'sir.' I tell them, 'There's no need for that, but if you insist, then please continue.'"

Unlike some of the palatial lofts I visited in Europe, the queen's lofts are not what one would call luxurious. The birds live in a simple wooden shed in Carlo's backyard. The only way one can tell the queen's pigeons apart from another's are the birds' race bands. The queen's bands are initialed "ER," for Elizabeth Regina. And no, they are not bejeweled.

On race day, I help pack the queen's birds into wicker baskets labeled H. M. QUEEN and ferry them to the club in King's Lynn, a low-lying town prone to periodic flooding. We drive past the town's central square, where, according to local legend, a witch was burned at the stake.

A small plaque on the second story of a building across the street marks the spot where her heart allegedly landed after exploding from her blistering chest.

Inside the club, members are already "on the piss" —knocking back pints of draft. As a rare guest, I am the recipient of friendly inquiries, free beers, and bawdy humor. To the amusement of club members, a young woman named Tina, affectionately referred to as the club's mascot, playfully shakes her cleavage into my reddening face. Another member turns to me and reveals his unsolicited secret for winning races: "When they come home, I give me birds an herbal salt bath and chest massage. They loves it, they do."

The next day I join Carlo and several friends in his backyard clubhouse, a small shed with a sliding glass door facing the loft. As we sit and wait for the birds to come home, Carlo, dressed in green sweatpants and a white undershirt, pours some Scotch and hands out cheap cigars. I help him cart out his television to watch a soccer tournament during the lull. A long extension cord snakes its way across the backyard.

A heavy rain begins to fall, which Carlo assumes will further discourage his birds from flying across the Wash. Although his birds' expected time of arrival comes and goes, Carlo won't take his eyes off the swollen sky, remarking that it's "a bit like watching the paint dry, isn't it?" Nearly an hour later, a shivering bird slowly lands on the loft. In due time, it is followed by several others. The race is a total loss. The birds most likely flew around the Wash.

★   ★   ★

The Belgians first concocted the sport of racing pigeons in the early nineteenth century. As pigeon couriers were gradually replaced by the telegraph, Belgians found another useful application for the birds: sport gambling. They transported the birds—often by a combination of foot and carriage—from Belgium to Paris, a distance of about 350 kilometers.

The sport rapidly increased in popularity, reaching its peak after World War II, when a quarter million Belgians—or roughly one in nine families—raced pigeons and kept a backyard loft. At the time, the average Belgian was lower-middle-class and had few of the distractions that we take for granted today, such as cars, television, and easy travel. Pigeon racing was an inexpensive and convenient way for them to get out of the house, drink beers with friends, and indulge in a little gambling. Wives were generally left at home to simmer in resentment at their absentee husbands.

Back then, lofts were modest affairs with a handful of birds. The races were short, generally under two hundred kilometers. Fanciers trained their birds by bicycle, riding ten kilometers into the countryside and releasing them from small baskets. Pigeon racing became the national sport of Belgium, with racecourse weather reports crowding the airwaves and race results published in the following day's newspapers.

As European workers grew more affluent, pigeon racing suffered. Families now had cars and could afford vacations and dinner out. Pigeon racing takes daily commitment, and in today's world of virtual hobbies, such as video games and spectator sports, who wants to clean coops and run around transporting pigeons?

To gauge the current state of affairs of international pigeon racing, I traveled to Belgium's Natural Granen Company (or "Natural"), of Antwerp, the oldest and largest company that deals exclusively in pigeon racing products. A family business, Natural was started by two young brothers who excelled at pigeon racing. They began with a successful journal in 1930, and six years later they started selling feed formulated for racing pigeons, which they advertised in their magazine.

I met with Joseph De Scheemaecker, son and nephew of the two founders. A trim man with a gray goatee, Joseph is in the process of handing over the company to his son Stephan. The granary and product warehouses are in an industrial area beside one of Antwerp's shipping canals. Since Belgium is the center of pigeon racing commerce, Natural's two main former competitors, also family-owned, used to do business just down the street. A sign of the times, both were bought up by pet food conglomerates, which then minimized their pigeon operations.

Although Natural grosses about $20 million a year, Joseph works out of a modest office filled with pigeon portraits and maps of China. When I ask him about business and the future of pigeon racing, he takes a deep sigh. Racing is a dying sport in Belgium, he tells me. Fanciers number just forty thousand, and 50 percent of them are over sixty. The attrition rate is about twenty-five hundred members a year. "It's a big problem," Joseph says. "A big, big problem." He ticks off numbers for other European nations: Britain has just 40,000 fanciers; France, 18,000; Holland, 34,000; and Germany, 60,000. Pigeon racing in eastern Europe, with its burgeoning middle class, is on a slight upswing.

But like western Europe, the United States pigeon community is also atrophying, with fewer than 15,000 racers scattered across the country, down from a postwar high of 40,000. They range from immigrant racers, like many of Orlando's competitors in New York City, to rural mid-westerners. It's the midwesterners who typically show up for the sport's annual convention, located each year in a different city, and which features, among other things, a ladies' auxiliary meeting and occasional polka dances.

The dwindling numbers are a mixed blessing for Natural. A deteriorating market can also mean diminished competition. Fanciers in these countries still need products, and Natural is well positioned to corner the market. The company exports its products—feeds, medicines, perches, dung scrapers, vitamins—to forty-four countries, including Kuwait, Argentina, and the Canary Islands. "Export is everything," Joseph tells me. "Today in Belgium, pigeon racing is more about business than sport. We are the number one export country for pigeon products."

Joseph gives me an extensive tour of his business, beginning with the granary, where thousands of kilos of feed are sorted, mixed, and packaged each day. The grains, which come from as far away as Africa and Asia, make their way through an array of clanking mechanical behemoths. They end up in fifty-pound bags printed in one of fifteen languages, including Hungarian, Greek, Arabic, and Turkish. They are then stacked on pallets and packed into shipping containers for worldwide distribution. "This order is for Romania," Joseph says, pointing at several large pallets. "This is for America. And this shipment is for Argentina—it's not so big, because they are having economic problems, yes?"

We walk over to the relative quiet of Natural's thirty-thousand-square-foot warehouse, where the company stores its pigeon accessories. Nearly every accessory in the building is made in China. "They all used to be made in Belgium, but no more," Joseph explains. "The unions are too strong here. They sell the workers dreams. Dreams! So now China gets all the business. And look how nicely they package everything, and for so little money. It's impressive, don't you think?"

We get into Joseph's car and drive to his stud farm, Natural's ninety-thousand-square-foot breeding facilities. On the way, Joseph expresses his doubts about the company's two hundred different varieties of feed formulas manufactured in the granary. "It's too much. Crazy, really. I only use one kind of feed, and it's our least expensive. But the customers demand it, especially the Germans. We lose markets if we don't sell them dreams. Our business is up because of these nonsense mixtures. The price is higher. The profit is higher. And the fancier is happier. Imagine."

The breeding facility houses about fifteen thousand pigeons, so many that it takes five employees one full week to vaccinate them all. Natural sells thirty thousand newborns a year, all of which are ordered before the egg is even laid. The birds live in row after row of open-air sheds that resemble an army's field quarters.

Natural targets the working class, rather than the minority of wealthy—and perhaps foolish—fanciers who often pay thousands of dollars for a bird with a champion lineage. Joseph's birds cost about $20 apiece, and he is painfully candid about what he is selling. The birds are bred from thirty well-respected strains, or documented bloodlines, but that's where the certainty ends. "We produce a lot of pigeons. Some are very good; many more are bad. We can only guarantee the health of the bird and its origin. It's like buying a lottery ticket. If the ticket is cheap enough, it's worth the risk."

In its own way, pigeon racing is a meritocracy. You can spend a lot of money on an expensive pigeon, but that alone won't ensure success. There is no guarantee whatsoever that a champion bird will pass on its vitality to its progeny. And even if it does, it will be wasted unless properly nurtured in the hands of a hardworking and knowledgeable fancier. Money is no substitute for dedication, which is why many of the world's top racers are elderly pensioners with decades of experience.

As Joseph concedes, Belgium is no longer a mecca for pigeon racing. But it does remain the sport's spiritual and commercial center. In effect, the country is cashing in on its faded glory. Wherever you go in the world, you'll find pigeon fanciers breeding Belgian birds and using Belgian products.

Nowhere is this more the case than in Asia, where a trip to Belgium is considered a mandatory pilgrimage. While Natural has its share of awed tourists, the *ne plus ultra* is a visit to the beating heart of competitive pigeon racing—a modest town house in the otherwise unremarkable Belgian village of Arendonck.

There resides Louie Janssen, an impish old man who sits on a genetic gold mine—the bloodline of his eponymous birds. Established and bred by his father in the 1930s and nurtured by Louie and his now deceased brothers, the pedigreed lineage of the Janssen birds is synonymous with speed and vitality. These birds are considered avian royalty, and their descendants can be found in tens of thousands of lofts across the globe. Framed portraits of Louie have been known to adorn the walls of many clubhouses in China, in the honorary space traditionally left for Communist leaders.

Although the Janssen siblings were made wealthy by their birds, they never married and never left the confines of their parents' home. Like many Belgians, they've always kept their birds in an attic loft and a small shed in their postage-stamp-sized backyard. Nobody's quite sure of the extent of the Janssen fortune—they've always demanded cash, which they've seemingly never spent. It is said that Louie has never traveled ten miles beyond his village. As he has no children, it's uncertain what he will do with the family fortune. It's rumored that he will donate it to his local church—that is, if the state doesn't confiscate it as compensation for decades of presumed tax evasion.

Residents of Arendonck are accustomed to bewildered pilgrims asking for directions in foreign tongues to the Janssen home. Louie greets them genially at his doorstep and agrees to pose for photographs. But it doesn't take long for the conversation to turn to business. Inevitably, the foreign fanciers want to know one thing: Are any of Louie's miraculous pigeons for sale?

Louie responds in a mischievous fashion that all too many pilgrims mistake for sincerity: "Gosh, I'm sorry, but no." The desperate visitors beg, plead, cajole: "Just one bird, any bird . . . *please!*" Thousands of dollars later, Louie descends from his attic loft, bird in hand, and "reluctantly" hands it to the grateful visitor, who is certain he just engineered an avian coup.

It's worth noting that Louie hasn't raced his birds for decades. Like Joseph De Scheemaecker at Natural and so many other Belgians, he's merely cashing in on Asia's pigeon mania. Incidentally, Joseph has also stopped pigeon racing. He lets his employees do it for him. And his son, the international corporate executive, has no interest in racing pigeons whatsoever.

Other Belgians are profiting from their nationality as well. Belgian racing magazines are translated into multiple languages (including Chinese), and Belgian veterinarians, some specializing exclusively in racing pigeons, analyze blood and fecal samples from around the world. When it comes to a valuable racing homer, droppings are shipped to a specialist at the slightest cause for concern.

China is the fastest-growing market for pigeon racing products, which would explain why Joseph's office is filled with maps of China. Nobody knows for sure how many pigeon racers there are in China, but most agree the number is in the hundreds of thousands and steadily increasing. As the country's living standards have risen, the sport has become more lucrative and competitive. But Joseph says he finds the Chinese market elusive. China's economic boom aside, many fanciers are peasants with just a handful of birds. "In China, they carry their birds to races in cardboard boxes, like we did sixty years ago," Joseph explains. "It is an emerging market."

But Taiwan and Japan are already fertile markets. Natural exports fifty industrial shipping containers of product a year to Taiwan alone. Pigeon racing has reached such a frenzied level there that it's not unusual for a fancier to bet $50,000 on a bird in one race, and for first-place race winnings to exceed $3 million. Lofts typically have several investor/owners as well as a professional loft manager and a trainer. Huge sums are paid for victorious birds, which are purchased for breeding and social status. In 1994 a Japanese businessman bought a long-distance champion racer from a French breeder for €200,000.

Joseph tells me that the Frenchman was a laid-off factory worker and widowed father of two young daughters. He had a knack for training birds and was reluctant to sell "Super Ben" to the Japanese businessman, who had shown up one day unannounced. The daughters convinced their father that a bird in hand was nothing compared to cash in hand. After all, homers live precarious lives. Although Super Ben survived his racing days without succumbing to hawks and other dangers, he narrowly escaped another grisly fate—the dinner plate. The bird was inexplicably left behind when a hungry thief raided the loft and made off with and later ate three quarters of the Frenchman's pigeons.

Because of such high valuations, a rash of pigeon kidnappings has plagued Taiwan and Japan. Bands of criminals routinely capture birds in long nets constructed along a race flyway. It's not uncommon for a ransom note to be accompanied by a severed pigeon foot. To adapt to this menace, organizers no longer publicize race times or locations. Often the birds are released from ships far out at sea, away from the reach of netters, and some home lofts have more security apparatus than Area 51.

In an attempt to revive the sport in the West, some racing organizations are pushing long-distance contests with larger cash prizes. One such race, the Barcelona, attracts tens of thousands of pigeon entries. The birds are released in Spain and fly five hundred–plus miles to their home lofts across northern Europe. Competition at these mega-races is fierce, and the stakes are high. Cheating has become a problem, and at some races, pigeons are tested for anabolic steroids and other doping. A winning bird attracts a near-devotional following. Besides prize money and side bets, a fancier can make thousands more studding the champion or selling him outright.

There are still many European fanciers who shun these long-distance races as nothing but hype and hooey. Any fancier with enough money to enter a bird can get lucky and win once, they complain. But what about the fancier who wins the local race week after week? Isn't he the real hero, the true backbone of the sport?

Frank Tasker is one such traditionalist. He lives just north of the Wash, not far from the town of Boston, ancestral home to many of America's early Puritan settlers. He considers the long-distance races nothing but plain old endurance tests and a sure way to send a good bird to an early death. He has even more contempt for another race innovation, the so-called one-loft races such as the Sun City Million Dollar Pigeon Race in South Africa and other races run out of Las Vegas and California. Newborn birds are mailed to a central racing loft, where they are all trained together so they all race back to the same loft. All the owner does is show up on the day of the race and hopefully leave with a big check.

Frank can't imagine handing over one of his babies to a stranger to care for and train, let alone for promises of financial gain. As far as he's concerned, these races violate the spirit of the sport. "I want to be the bird's owner, its trainer and jockey," he says. "These birds are athletes of the highest order. Each race is a serious competition."

A former butcher with an unruly mop of white hair and an uncanny resemblance to Newt Gingrich, Frank is arguably the finest pigeon racer in all of England. His birds take top honors in race after race. His best bird earned twenty-one first prizes and was twice named Britain's top pigeon for races up to 250 miles. Suffice to say, Frank has spent many successful years squinting at the sky for his pigeons. But winning that often has its drawbacks. Frank has decimated his local competition and made some enemies along the way.

Frank recently returned from China, where he was on pigeon business, to find that half of his local racing club's membership had mutinied and formed another club. Their first order of business was ensuring that Frank could never become a member. All members had to live within certain geographical boundaries, and surprise, surprise, Frank's house fell short of the residency requirement by a few hundred yards.

Of all the pigeon people I've met, Frank tops the list when it comes to obsession. During the racing season, hardly a minute goes by when Frank isn't feeding, exercising, or handling his birds. He's with them from dawn to dusk. He lies in bed thinking about them until he falls asleep, and then he dreams about them. Come morning, he jumps out of bed, throws on his coaching sweats, places a whistle around his neck, and runs off to exercise his birds. "I can't visualize a morning without pigeons," he tells me. "I think such a life would be rather empty."

I spent two grueling days with Frank at the height of the racing season, and by the end I was overwhelmed by his fanaticism. Although he was charming and hospitable, I found myself chasing after him the entire time as he performed various tasks. I felt nothing but empathy for his wife, Ann, and pigeon widows the world over. Just as Ann was continually forced to reheat dinner when Frank's promised arrival was delayed, so, too, were my promised interviews, travel research, and networking introductions put off, rescheduled, and dropped.

If Frank wasn't busy brewing herbal tea (with fresh lavender) for the pigeons, he was administering eyedrops and giving them vitamin supplements. If he wasn't cleaning the coops (twice a day) and checking the filtered water, he was exercising the birds.

The cocks were let out for an hour of circular flying from seven to eight A.M. The hens were let out from eight to nine A.M. The young hens and cocks were let out from noon to four P.M. Another set of cocks was let out from five to six P.M., and a set of hens was exercised from six to seven P.M. Other birds were packed up and driven out of town and then released. And then there was a visit to the clubhouse to drop off the race birds, followed by two hours of inputting club data into the computer.

When Frank finally did sit down for dinner, the phone would ring, and he'd gossip about the upcoming race with the caller. I sat with Ann in the kitchen, both of us waiting patiently for a few moments of Frank's complete and undivided attention. A normally vivacious woman with a sharp wit, Ann stared at me with a look of utter resignation.

"It's a selfish sport," she tells me. "It's always been about the birds. We never went on holiday. We never went out on weekends. Our children resented him. He was always too busy with the birds to spend time with [the kids]. If only he'd have taken us out Sundays, or even every other

Sunday . . . Back then a big day out meant packing the kids and the dog in the car, driving thirty miles, and releasing the birds. Then we'd simply drive back.

"When he turned sixty, he promised he'd cut down on the number of birds he kept and spend more time with me. He said we'd go on holiday more. And I believed him! It wasn't two months later that he expanded the loft . . . All he wants to do is talk about pigeons, pigeons, pigeons. I *hate* when every conversation veers off and ends up being about pigeons. But I guess when you marry a pigeon man, it comes with the territory."

Frank catches the tail end of the conversation and is seemingly oblivious to its significance. "I'm thinking about pigeons twenty-four hours a day," he says jovially. "I only got one life to live, and I want to spend mine racing pigeons!"

From Orlando to Frank to the rising stars of Asia, the sport fascinates and titillates. But this obsession clearly comes at a steep price—neglect for all things deemed tangential to winning, such as maintaining the semblance of a normal family life. While many will argue that a generational interest in pigeons has united their family in powerful ways, I suspect that just as many would wring the birds' little necks if given half the chance. In fact, they would probably be envious of my next journey—into the bloody viscera of the squab industry, where speed and endurance are associated with one's knife skills, and where celebrating pigeons is more a matter of . . . taste.

12

The Breast Farm

And the priest shall bring [the dove] unto the altar,
and wring off his head . . . it is a burnt sacrifice, an
offering made by fire, of a sweet savor unto the Lord.
                                        —Leviticus 1:15–17

Most people, once having eaten squab, desire to eat it
again.
                —Wendell Levi, "Making Pigeons Pay"

IF YOU ASK THE WORLD'S TOP CHEFS WHAT THEIR FAVORITE meat is, many of them will tell you squab. Unlike much bland white-meat poultry, squab is a dark, moist, delicate, and oh-so-tender flesh that can be served rare enough to melt in your mouth. A chef can demand rich sums for squab, a Scandinavian derivative for "fat and tender." But call it pigeon, and diners will avoid it like the plague.

Just as veal comes from young calves that have barely exercised their legs, squab comes from month-old pigeons that have never spread their wings. They're plump with baby fat that hasn't hardened into muscle. Older pigeons are edible but require more cooking to soften the meat.

Throughout human history, squab has been considered a delicacy. The pharaohs feasted on it, as did Roman emperors and the kings and queens of Europe. For hundreds of years, European nobility relied on their dove-cotes to supply them with a year-round source of protein.

While squab has remained fashionable in Europe and Asia, its popularity in America has ebbed and flowed. For centuries, American farmers harvested the squabs roosting in their barns. Back then, unless you lived in a city, protein was what you could hunt, and pigeon was easy—all you had to do was reach up and grab the babies.

As seen with the overhunting of the passenger pigeon, pigeon meat was enormously popular. It was stewed, roasted, or made into the once ubiquitous pigeon potpie. But when the government began regulating game hunting in the late nineteenth century, wild fowl such as pheasant and quail were harder to come by in large quantities, making the easily farmed pigeon even more popular.

Squab farming became one of America's favorite get-rich-quick schemes. Thousands of poor Americans believed the easy-money propaganda disseminated by hucksters looking to sell breeders, loft supplies, and how-to manuals. But once they bought in to the business, they found raising pigeons harder than throwing feed into a trough and waiting for eggs to hatch. The markets became glutted besides.

It wasn't until the rise of industrial chicken farming that squab's popularity took a hit. For years, chickens were looked upon as curiosities, considered difficult to raise, prone to predators, and utilized mainly for their eggs. But as poultry farming turned into a science, chickens flew past pigeons in prominence. Squab became a richer man's meal, which conveyed a certain status upon its diners. Even today, while squab fetches as much as $8 a pound, chicken retails for under a dollar. And it keeps getting cheaper: Chicken today costs half of what it did sixty years ago.

Cost, as well as the bird's recent defamation, has turned the squab industry into niche marketers in the specialty foods arena, similar to goat meat farmers. They pursue fancier white-tablecloth restaurants and the expanding Asian immigrant population, which prefers dark meat because it is more flavorful. The Chinese view squab as a celebratory banquet food that brings good luck, happiness, and prosperity (it's considered an honor to eat the head). The majority of America's squab production ends up in Chinatowns across the country.

The Palmetto Pigeon Plant in Sumter, South Carolina, is one of the nation's oldest and biggest squab farms. Sumter has a deserted downtown; a commercial strip filled with national chains; Shaw Air Force Base, the area's largest employer; and the pigeon plant. And that's about it.

In late July, the weather is ungodly hot and humid. Sumter, and much of South Carolina in general, has the unique disposition of looking as if the ocean is nearby when it isn't. It has all the characteristics of shore topography: The land is flat as roadkill, the soil is loamy, and the trees are piney. But since the seashore is over two hours away, the city reaps none of the benefits. Instead of cooling ocean breezes and endless vistas, Sumter is filled with mosquitoes, breezeless humidity, and swampy water.

The pigeon plant is located on the commercial strip and beside a lawn sign that reads: ONLY JESUS FORGIVES SINNERS. When the plant first opened in 1923, this was farm country; cotton was king, and the plant was one of the few production-oriented employers. Three southern

Jews opened the plant: two brothers and their friend, the famed (at least in pigeon circles) Wendell Levi. At the time, dozens of large squab farms and processing plants dotted the American landscape. Now there's just Palmetto and three competitors out west.

Tony Barwick, a former employee who studied poultry science in college and dreamed of owning his own poultry plant one day, bought the business twenty years ago. A large, friendly man in his forties, Tony isn't particularly interested in the rich history of the animals he slaughters daily. "It's just a bird," he tells me. "This is a business. We're producing animals for meat." Speed, endurance, and delicately stenciled wing bars mean nothing to Tony. All he cares about are breasts, because that's where the meat is. "I want nice, well-rounded ones," he tells me. "I want big breasts."

Tony has no illusions about the value of his birds. They don't have racing pedigrees with owners hoping to sell them for thousands of dollars at auction. Tony harvests his pigeons like vegetables and sells them by the pound. Palmetto raises utility birds, larger breeds of rock doves with big, broad chests. He keeps sixty thousand on hand for breeding and slaughters about seven thousand of the babies a week. "Business is good," Tony says. "More and more celebrity chefs are turning people on to squab. But it'll never be like chicken. God designed the chicken to feed the world." (Factory farming presumably did the rest.)

Tony expects his animals to work for a living: He wants his breeders to be breeding and his squabs to be eating. "The squabs are basically twenty-four-hour feed manufacturing units," he explains as we walk past row after row of open-air coops just behind his office. "They are converting feed to meat. That's their role: to convert it as soon as possible. The sooner they do that, the sooner we can get them into production."

We enter one of the dozens of wood and wire coops that date back to 1923. Take away the heat and humidity, and I could just as easily be touring Natural's Belgian breeding farm. Tony picks up a young chick and turns it over. The baby, with its prominent beak and sparsely feathered body, doesn't put up much of a struggle. "You see this?" Tony asks, pointing to the bird's nearly transparent belly. "That's food up here, food it's just eaten. And this here is food digesting. And this? That's poop waiting to come out. This guy should be ready for processing in about two weeks. We try to pull 'em out just before their parents' push them out. At about four weeks."

We walk over to the adjacent processing plant. Tony introduces me to Christie, his sister and plant manager. She looks at my sandals and suggests I change into hardier footwear. A former veterinary technician, Christie now supervises the slaughter of animals. "It was weird at first, but you get used to it," she tells me. "Now I can go on the killing floor and it's just second nature."

Inside the plant, Christie opens a cabinet and hands me a white apron used by workers in the evisceration room. Workers on the "kill floor" wear red smocks for reasons you might suspect. We walk around the building and up a short flight of stairs to the kill floor. Crates of birds are stacked on the loading dock, peacefully awaiting their execution. But just inside the door, it's total avian pandemonium.

Two men pull the birds from their crates and swiftly stuff them upside down into two rows of metal funnels. The birds' heads stick out of the small opening on the bottom, and their feet dangle above them. A worker named Reggie takes a knife and slits all their throats. The birds bleed into a trough below. As they bleed out—a process that takes anywhere from thirty to ninety seconds—the birds twitch, either voluntarily or involuntarily, depending on the precision of Reggie's cut.

Like an image out of some dime-store novel, a snow-white pigeon escapes its crate and lands in the bloody trough. Coated in spurting blood and unsure where to go, it paces back and forth aimlessly, much like the escaped pigeons at the Pennsylvania gun club.

There's blood everywhere. It splatters the workers, and it pools on the floor an inch deep. After bleeding out, the dead or nearly dead birds are tossed en masse into a steaming cauldron of piping-hot water that loosens their feathers. Next they are thrown into a centrifuge covered with knobby rubber "fingers" that remove the feathers. Then the babies are tossed down a chute to land in the evisceration room.

After a day of killing, Reggie steps outside for a smoke. "I know how to catch them by the neck and cut 'em just right," he tells me. "After a while you get real fast at it." Christie informs me that Palmetto does all of its processing the old-fashioned way—by hand. "That way we can give each bird a little more individual attention."

We walk around to the evisceration room, which contains about forty employees. The laborers, Reggie included, are all black, just as Christie and the rest of the front office are all white. "We had some whites," Christie informs me. "But they didn't get along well with the blacks." One of the first things Tony did when he started working at the plant in 1987 was integrate the bathrooms.

The large windowless evisceration room is organized into an assembly line. Clumps of naked birds coming down the chute from the kill floor are immediately hung upside down on a conveyor belt of hangers suspended from the ceiling. The birds swing by their feet to the various stations of disembowelment. Christie walks me through the process. On one occasion, I feel her tapping me on my shoulder. But when I turn around, I realize it's a gutted pigeon swinging around on the conveyor.

"Now, this here is what we call the rosebud," Christie explains. We watch as a woman cuts an incision across a bird's bunghole. It reveals a bunched-up length of curlicued intestine that has a flower-like appearance. "Now, you don't want to cut too deep. If you puncture the intestines, fecal might come out. You don't want a bird leaving here with fecal. Fecal contaminates everything."

We watch as two women pull out the birds' guts and hang them on the conveyor belt. Next we visit Maybelle, the crop puller. Christie takes a bird and explains the anatomy of a pigeon's throat. "Now, this right here, that's the windpipe. You see?" The birds' crops still have undigested feed in them. Many of these pigeons were eating right up until the moment they were selected for slaughter.

Next it's the lung pullers' turn. "These right here are the lungs," Christie says, pointing to a small mass of pale flesh on the floor. "You see that?" The livers, hearts, and gizzards are saved and thrown into large tubs, where they are processed and then thrown back into a bird that's not necessarily their original owner.

"This here is the finished product," Christie says, holding up a slab of naked flesh that bears little resemblance to the doves I saw on the loading dock. "Look up there, up in the cavity. Everything's gone: heart, lungs, crop, everything. And there's no fecal. If we find some, then the bird gets reworked."

With the gutting complete, the workers scrub the area spotless with chlorine and empty the bins of viscera. "We don't chunk anything," Christie explains, using a rural southern term for "throw away." "All the blood, the guts . . . it gets picked up and taken to a rendering plant."

We walk over to the packaging area, where each bird is vacuum-packed and then tossed into a blast freezer. The final product is a little oval package no bigger than a softball.

When I walk back to Tony's office, he directs me into the company kitchen, where he opens up an oven and pulls out a tray of roasted squab breasts. He has prepared fresh squab breasts for me using his favorite recipe. He marinates them in soy sauce and ginger, bakes them, and finishes them off under the broiler so the skin is crispy.

It's barely ten minutes since I left the kill and evisceration rooms, and frankly I'm not in the mood to consume *any* animal. But after a lifetime of avoiding eating little birds, I'm determined to try Tony's squab.

I pick up a breast with a drumstick attached to it. It's about the size of a small chicken thigh. The meat is low in fat and high in protein, although the skin is fatty, like that of duck, Tony informs me. With a dripping breast still in my hand, I watch him munch away on pigeon. "I just looooove it," he tells me in a slow drawl. He picks up another piece, dunks it back in the cooking juices, and then puts the whole thing in his mouth.

Hesitantly, I take a small bite. I feel a bit queasy, but . . . it *is* tasty. The meat is dark and flavorful, and Tony did a nice job on the marinade. I take another bite— then reach for another breast.

Pigeon Pot Pie

Ingredients

6 pigeons, gutted and cleaned
4 tbsp. butter, separated
Salt and pepper
1 onion, chopped
10 cloves of garlic, minced
1 carrot, sliced
1 celery stalk, sliced
1 handful parsley, chopped
Splash of white wine
½ cup flour
2 pastry shells, uncooked

Directions:

Sauté pigeons in two tablespoons of butter, searing both sides. Sprinkle with salt and pepper.

Add a half-cup of water to sauté pan. Add onion, garlic, carrot, parsley, celery, and splash of wine. Cover and simmer until tender.

Remove pigeons and debone the meat. Add flour and rest of butter to the broth. Simmer until thickened.

Grease a pie pan and then fill with a pastry shell. Add the meat and the thickened broth. Cover with the other pastry shell. Bake at 350 degrees until browned.

Enjoy with a nice bottle of wine.

Autumn

13

The Main Event

ORLANDO'S OBSESSIVE TRAINING SCHEDULE PAYS OFF HAND-
somely come fall as his birds dominate the young-bird
club races. By the time it's shipping night for the Main
Event in mid-October, Orlando's birds have placed first
in six races. In one race, they even won a trifecta—first,
second, and third place.

Shipping night for the Main Event is a once-a-year
celebration. The Bronx Homing Pigeon Club is swamped
with people, food, and chatter. A giant foil-wrapped buf-
fet is representative of the night's diversity: rice and beans,
stuffed peppers and manicotti, fried chicken and greens,
kielbasa and sauerkraut.

Outside in the clubhouse garage, racers from
Queens, Brooklyn, Staten Island, New Jersey, Long Island, and Connecticut drop off their birds to be shipped
all the way to Triadelphia, West Virginia, over 350 miles
away. The club's vice president inspects each bird's wings
to make sure they have molted properly. Molting uses up
a tremendous amount of a bird's energy, so some racers
try to retard the molting process by keeping their birds in
the dark for at least sixteen hours a day. That way the birds
can put all their energy into racing. But it's cheating, so a

bird's wings are checked for proper molting before it's allowed to race.

Another man inspects all the race clocks, synchronizes them, and then seals them. In the center of the room, people place additional bets on the race through an auctioning process. For example, if someone thinks Orlando's birds will do especially well, he or she can "buy" the loft. If one of Orlando's birds wins, the bettor will also win a substantial sum.

Back inside, the organizers of the race, Joey Musto and Larry Doherty, collect funds and officially enter contestants into the race. Musto, a boiler mechanic who serves as race secretary, speaks with a voice so gravelly it could pave a driveway. Doherty, a sprightly Irish gentleman of seventy-three, wears an old-fashioned newsboy cap and has buttoned his shirt all the way to the top.

Doherty is busy discussing the litter he uses—"crushed corncob mixed with feathers and droppings, raked daily, to provide a natural warmth in the coop"—when nineteen-year-old Jason Howel of Staten Island walks up to pay his entry fee. Howel is easily two decades younger than the other racers milling about.

"There aren't too many young guys going into it," says Howel, who races with his uncle. "None of my friends want anything to do with it. But I like it. I spend twelve hours a day with the birds. It keeps me out of trouble." The amount of time racing requires also keeps Howel from going to college. "Everything's for the birds. It's got to be like that if you want to win," he says.

"It's not a sport that attracts a lot of young people these days," Doherty says. "I started flying pigeons when I was ten. I learned from my father, who flew pigeons in the old country. But I have eight children and seventeen grandchildren, and not one of them is interested in it. More kids graduate college nowadays than win races." The club's membership roster has dwindled from eighty, when Doherty joined in 1956, to its current thirty-five.

"It's endless work, three hundred sixty-five days a year," pipes up Donna Musto, Joe's wife, from across the table. "To be honest, I don't get it. He's always with the birds, and when he's not, they're always on his mind. We plan our vacations around them, our nights out around them. He's like, 'We can't go out tonight—it's pigeon night.' Hell, we plan everything around them. It's like they're his babies. And it only gets worse during training. It's always pigeons, pigeons, pigeons. It's all I hear. Fifteen years later, I can't even look at them anymore. Meanwhile, he's up on the roof, in that raining weather, waiting for those damn birds to come home."

Musto throws Donna a look reminiscent of Jackie Gleason in *The Honeymooners* and then asks her to "go get the picture." Donna doesn't budge. Musto grudgingly gets up and returns with a Polaroid. He slides it across the table.

The photo is of a pigeon standing on a pedestal, looking blankly into the camera. "Out of two thousand and forty-eight birds, she comes in first!" Musto says excitedly. "First! It's something I never done before." Musto folds his arms across his barrel chest and beams.

"See, he had to tell you," Donna says. "He had to show you the picture."

Doherty chimes in. "I'm married fifty years, and I told my wife that as long as we have the blue check hen upstairs, we're okay." Most everyone in the room laughs. Doherty's best breeder is a blue check hen.

"When you breed birds, you put all your hopes in them," Doherty continues. "To breed future winners, that's an aspiration we all have . . . To see that bundle of sixteen ounces fly home from three hundred miles away just to come back to what you've been giving it . . . it satisfies everything. She came home!"

The next day, nearly a year after my first visit with Orlando, I am standing on his Brooklyn rooftop squinting into the crisp October sky. The weather is absolutely gorgeous. In one direction, you can see the leaves changing colors in Prospect Park. In the other, the Manhattan skyline shines brilliantly. Omayra fidgets on a lawn chair nearby, eating fried chicken. It smells delicious, and it's making me hungry.

But Orlando's attention is drawn elsewhere—to a relatively bland vista of Newark and Staten Island. Today is the Main Event, and somewhere out there, Orlando's homing pigeons are furiously pumping their wings, relying on internal compasses to catapult themselves home from West Virginia at 60 mph. They should be jetting across Staten Island any moment now, pinpointing their loft from thousands of feet above and hundreds of miles away with the precision of a laser-guided missile. Then again, a laser-guided missile has an unfair advantage—it knows from where it's been launched. These birds have never been to West Virginia before.

Orlando paces nervously around the roof. With a cell phone at one ear and a cordless phone at the other, he looks a bit like My Favorite Martian, with twin antennas rising from his head.

After a season of intensive training, Orlando knows exactly what it will take for him to win—a bird that won't stop for water, food, or even bad weather. Hundreds of pigeon racers are scanning the horizon today from rooftops across New York City, New Jersey, and Long Island, just like Orlando, waiting for their feathered athletes to fly home. They're in constant contact with one another, their cell phones chirping incessantly. News of a sighting heads west to east from rooftop to rooftop.

Orlando's cell phone rings again, to the tune of Ravel's *Boléro*. Rumors of a sighting at a competitor's rooftop loft in Queens have Orlando on edge. But after a careful study of weather charts, Orlando is convinced his birds won't start arriving for another fifteen minutes. He has every reason to believe his little minions will lead the pack today, as they have for much of the season. "I'm kicking so much ass this year, people think I'm using steroids," he tells me. "Meanwhile, I'm waking up at four-thirty in the morning to train." I struggle to imagine Orlando waking up before most everyone else is already at work.

The cell phone and the cordless handset ring in quick succession. "I haven't seen a thing, not a thing," Orlando shouts into the cell phone before turning his attention to the cordless. "You can never tell with the Main Event," he shouts. "Anything can happen."

I squint at the horizon. It's filled with dark specks: distant planes, insects, sparrows, seagulls, starlings, and optical illusions. And yet, somehow, Orlando can always tell when a distant speck is one of his pigeons racing home. He doesn't even flinch at the sight of a city pigeon a hundred yards away.

Orlando is feeling the race slip out of his control. His body is tense, like a shock absorber preparing to absorb a big blow. More rumors swirl that the sighting in Queens was real, and a telephone consensus is building that a bird did clock in at Bert & Harry Loft in Maspeth at 2:16 P.M.—just minutes ago.

"That's impossible!" Orlando shouts into the cell phone. "Well, it's not impossible, but that bird's supersonic. I got to go." Orlando switches to his cordless. "Unbelievable! Nobody else has birds. Are you sure you heard right? Something's wrong here. I want a congressional investigation! . . . What? One of Cosmo's birds?"

Dreams of winning the Main Event are fading fast. Orlando puts down the cordless, picks up a Chico—a bird that is thrown up to help guide the pigeons home once they are sighted—and scans the horizon. He dials the cell phone. "Yo, you heard? Bert and Harry got one at two-sixteen. I ain't kidding. Nobody else got shit. Bert and Harry are straight shooters, but I haven't seen a feather. Okay. Got to go."

The cell phone rings. It's Joey Musto from the Bronx. "You got two birds? Okay, okay. That's three so far." Orlando hangs up and scans west. Still no homers.

Omayra, wearing her lucky maroon sweatshirt, remains sitting patiently on her lawn chair, even though she says she's dying to call and have more fried chicken delivered. But she knows the rules: no unnecessary phone calls on race day, least of all the Main Event. The phone lines are conduits of critical race information and must be kept open at all times.

Ten more minutes pass. Orlando tries to make sense of the time discrepancies. He has already checked the weather online. "It's the Blue Ridge Mountains. They're tall, and it gets misty up there. Most birds don't like to cross it. They go back and forth trying to find a way around it. But some birds got balls. They go right through it. Bert and Harry's bird's got—" Orlando is suddenly speechless, frozen in place. "*Dios mío!*" shouts Omayra.

An exhausted-looking pigeon circles above. Orlando releases the Chico and races into position. The pigeon lands on the coop. Orlando approaches it, holding the giant flyswatters above him, and whistles tenderly. Omayra grabs a handful of Spanish peanuts and squats under the coop entrance, where she will grab the elastic race band off the pigeon's ankle.

Clocking is a critical element of winning. With hundreds of birds arriving at nearly the same time, every second counts. Orlando spends countless hours training his birds to hit the boards and go right into the coop above his bedroom closet.

Orlando continues his tender whistle, but the pigeon doesn't budge. "Come on, Mamí!" Orlando urges. "Come on!" The bird grooms itself and then looks away.

Orlando is about to hemorrhage. He can't wait any longer. Too much money and prestige are at stake. He traps the bird with the hooples. Omayra removes the race band, places it in a metal capsule, drops it, finds it again, and then sticks it in the clock, where it is time-stamped.

The clock reads 2:39 P.M. Orlando gets back on the phones and starts calling. Six more birds come in to Orlando's coop soon thereafter. "Quality shows," he boasts. "I bred a lot of winners this year." But in the end, his birds are far from winners—one comes in twenty-second, another in the mid-nineties, and the rest don't even rank. His boasts hollow, Orlando clams up, while Omayra phones in for some more fried chicken and plantains.

After a late lunch, Orlando sits down on a couch to digest his loss. "I thought I had the winners," he says. "But you can't get disappointed. Pigeon racing has a way of humbling you. Look, there are only two or three really big races a year, and I've been lucky enough to win my share of them. If I never win another, I've still done well."

Orlando gets up and starts pacing the room, growing more animated by the minute. "I'm going to do things differently next year," he says. "I'm going to start training them later and let them fly as a pack for a little longer. That way they won't get bored of the same routine. You see, the way I treat my birds and maintain their health, they can pull out of the pack. But they got to want to. It's up to me to motivate them. This year they got bored. That was the problem."

When Omayra leaves the room, Orlando lowers his voice and confesses his desire for an early retirement in Florida—not for the beaches but for the year-round pigeon racing. "There's a place called Spring Hill, Florida, about an hour from Tampa," he says. "They call it Little Belgium. It's where old pigeon fliers—the champions—go to die. The competition is unbelievable. And they race every day!

"Now, *that's* what I call living."

14

They Had No Choice

THE SIKH CUSTOMS OFFICER AT LONDON'S HEATHROW AIRport asks me what sort of business brings me to England.

"Pigeons," I say.

"Pigeons?" he repeats, incredulous.

"Yes. I'm attending a dinner at the Houses of Parliament celebrating pigeons."

It's only six A.M., but he is clearly amused. "Pigeon's on the menu, is it?" His eyes are tearing from laughter. His fellow customs officials heartily join him in his mirth.

When I first began writing this book, I expected looks of puzzlement, perhaps even bewilderment. After all, who would bother writing about pigeons? But the next night, there I am, standing under the impressively lit Big Ben alongside the Thames River. Beside me are many of my dinner companions, several dozen pigeon men and their wives. Like the pigeons we are here to celebrate, these men are considered commoners, mostly blue-collar laborers from the rural countryside, many with heavy northern accents that are difficult to understand.

Tonight they have left behind their usual work clothes and awkwardly donned suits and ties. Many of them are probably thinking what I'm thinking: How the hell did I get invited to the Houses of Parliament, let alone for a dinner honoring pigeons?

Tomorrow is England's annual Veterans Day, and tonight we are here to celebrate the recent building of a London memorial honoring pigeons, as well as the legions of other animals, that served alongside British soldiers throughout history. The monument's motto: "They had no choice."

Never mind that much of Parliament is tightly wrapped in netting designed to keep pigeons out, or that the mayor of London has declared war down the street on Trafalgar Square's "filthy flying rats," tonight the feral pigeon is the guest of honor at the very epicenter of British society. Squab, incidentally, is not on the menu.

After a private tour of both Houses of Parliament, our rather awed group is led to the Churchill Room beneath the House of Commons, where we dine beneath an austere portrait of the big man himself. We are the guests of Lord Tony Banks, a former sports minister in the Blair government, whose father was an avid pigeon racer. Also joining us are British football legend and mullet aficionado Gerry Francis, and several veterans of Britain's Ninth Parachute Battalion, which parachuted into Normandy on D-day.

I sit at a table with a champion racer who was recently put out of business by a pair of peregrine falcons who feasted on his homers. His wife is reserved, but I detect a note of glee in her voice as she describes a trip they have just taken to Malta—their first trip abroad in years—made possible, no doubt, by the hungry peregrines.

Also at the table is Dr. Jean Hansell, an elderly woman who has spent the past two decades of her retirement tirelessly advocating for pigeons and the architectural preservation of their dovecotes. A little knowledge goes a long way when it comes to gaining an appreciation for these birds, she tells me. "People just don't make the connection between the dove of peace and the pigeon in the street."

I had visited with Jean at her home in Bath earlier in the year, just after my trip to Sandringham. She had taken me on a field trip outside of town where we tromped through a field of overgrown stinging nettles to reach a neglected five-hundred-year-old dovecote with thick stone walls and a steep slate roof. Like many of England's two thousand dovecotes, the pigeon house was adjacent to a country estate, which in this case once belonged to the godson of Queen Elizabeth I.

Inside the floors were covered with several inches of droppings and the walls were lined with hundreds of pigeon cubbyholes. A soft light filtered in from an opening far above us in the center of the building's four gables. A white dove hovered on a rafter and then alit through the aperture.

Inhabited since well before the Romans, the city of Bath, like the many dovecotes that dot the landscape around it, has seen the rise and fall of countless gods, empires, and buildings. Most of them now lie buried under the ground, just like the famous Roman baths, for which the city is named. Although now excavated, they still sit nearly twenty feet below the modern city's surface.

And yet one feature of Bath has been left unchanged. As the city's fortunes ebbed and flowed with the surge of history—the pigeon has always remained. And this dovecote, with its occasional feathered visitors, is a testament to the bird's stubborn survival.

Back at the dinner, one of the veterans stands up and tells us about Duke of Normandy, the pigeon that saved his life on D-day. "We were to destroy four German hundred-and-ten-millimeter siege guns. We had trained a year for this mission. We were to put the guns out of action, which we did. But we were unsure of our communications and had to be sure to get a message to a naval cruiser that the guns had been destroyed. So our signaler turned to this poor pigeon that had been cooped up in a little canister for four days. He tied a message to the bird's leg and let him go. But he didn't go gracefully. The little guy staggered about and then flew toward Cannes in the wrong direction. Personally, I didn't know much about pigeons, and I could hardly believe that we were putting our lives in this bird's hands. But once the Duke got his bearings, away he went and delivered our message to the gunship. If it weren't for that bird, we would have been bombed, and I might not be here today."

Another of the night's speakers is Jim Jenner, a pigeon enthusiast and filmmaker from Montana who has dedicated much of his life to making educational documentaries about his favorite bird. "For the past fifty years, I've watched the total erosion of respect for the bird," Jim says. "One of the world's most revered creatures and one of nature's most phenomenal athletes has been reduced to the status of vermin in the minds of the general public."

Jenner is right, of course: Once a war hero, the feral pigeon is now the underdog of the animal kingdom. Not yet bullied into extinction like its ill-fated cousin the passenger pigeon, the unassuming bird is nonetheless persecuted daily. Unlike a prettily plumed parrot, a falcon with its dramatic flight and taloned profile, or a hummingbird with its tantalizingly delicate features and remarkable migrations, the ubiquitous pigeon's subtle charms are presumed, at best, mundane.

A day later, I stroll over to Trafalgar Square, in the heart of London, to see the pigeons. Beneath the towering column celebrating Admiral Nelson and his naval victory, there's a paucity of pigeons. I throw a few crusts of bread on the pavement to attract some birds across the way. (The sale of bird seed in the square is now banned.) A few rock doves approach but are quickly scared off by a tattooed man balancing a hooded falcon on his forearm. The man angrily stomps his feet at the pigeons and then picks up the crust.

"I wouldn't do that unless you want a fifty-euro fine," he tells me with a smirk. "Feeding the pigeons is illegal, you know. They spread disease. All sorts of disease."

A half hour later, he's gone and the birds are back. A playful toddler runs into the flock and cries out ecstatically when they take flight and flutter about. He stands there astonished by his own power and speechless at the beauty of the birds as they circle the Nelson column in formation and land nearby. He shrieks with laughter and runs toward them again.

I throw some more crusts and watch the subjects of my long journey rush toward me and gobble down the food. Something's different, at least for me. Where once I saw generic birds, now I see all sorts of variations. The birds, once just gray and blue, are now a subtle rainbow of patterned iridescent colors. I spot a handsome homer with a racing band around its ankle mingling with his feral brethren. Across the way, a male pigeon struts around with his tail feathers spread and lowered to the ground like a lobster tail. I recognize that he is courting the female pigeon beside him, who shows few signs of arousal.

I then stroll over to Hyde Park and the Animals in War memorial that we celebrated the night before. The monument consists of a large graceful wall carved with depictions of horses, mules, dogs, camels, and other "common" beasts of burden. At the behest of their human owners, they are dutifully marching forth into battle and harm's way.

In the far upper corner of the tableau are three rock doves—leading the charge.

Afterword

ABOUT A YEAR AFTER WRITING *PIGEONS*, I FOUND MYSELF walking around the city of St. Paul, Minnesota, looking for bird droppings. Accompanying me was Stephanie Boyles, a wildlife biologist for People for the Ethical Treatment of Animals, and Bob Kessler, a high-ranking mayoral aide.

A few months earlier, the mayor's car was crapped on. He pulled Kessler aside and demanded he find a solution to the city's so-called "pigeon problem." The mayor wasn't just concerned about his car; he was thinking ahead to the 2008 GOP Convention, when the eyes of the world would be on St. Paul. He didn't want his city seen as a splattered mess.

We found plenty of poo on the sidewalk and pigeons nesting above. St. Paul's pigeons have taken a liking to the city's skyways—enclosed second-story walkways that connect many of its buildings. Ever adaptable, the pigeons found the I-beams supporting the skyways to be perfect nesting areas.

Walking across these indoor sidewalks, I could see the birds huddled up against the glass, with the girders providing a cozy shelter for their nests and eggs. It was actually rather charming: How often does one get such a perfect bird's-eye view of a busy nest? I found myself wish-ing the eggs would hatch so I could see the fuzzy haired babies. Such a thing might once and for all dispel the urban myth that baby pigeons are invisible.

By big city standards, these birds hardly struck me as a momentous problem. But I had to hand it to St. Paul: they were about to become the first city in America to employ comprehensive humane pigeon control measures.

It's not as if the city hadn't experimented with every other possible method first, many of them brutal. Fifteen years earlier, another mayor hired a company to trap the birds and sell them to gun clubs for target practice. Not surprisingly, that pissed off a lot of people, and once again, pigeons somehow became front-page news. More recently, the city experimented with ultrasound devices to scare the birds away. But the pigeons adapted to the sound, or moved to neighboring perches.

"It's clear that the only way to make something work is for all the building owners downtown to cooper-ate together on this," Kessler tells me. "That means city hall, the cathedral, the state capital, and all the private landlords downtown, which would be a first. But if we don't, these birds are just going to hop from building to building."

Stephanie and I were there to help the city assess the problem and guide them through the PiCAS method used throughout much of Europe: a mixture of rooftop pigeon lofts for controlled breeding, deterrent measures, and public education about the drawbacks to overfeeding. Added to the mix is a new birth control–laced feed, called OvoControl, that makes the birds temporarily infertile, which Los Angeles began experimenting with as well to much fanfare.

The birth control method has found another new adherent: Ingrid Newkirk, founder of PETA. No matter how much she is educated about overfeeding the pigeons on her office balcony in Norfolk, Virginia, she apparently can't quit the habit.

If performed properly, St. Paul should reap plenty of benefits from its new pigeon-control measures, and with some luck, such measures will find their way around the country. It's not that hard of a sale: poisons, trappings, and the haphazard application of deterrent devices are expensive and simply don't work. A course of action premised on hatred is hardly a recipe for success. Sooner or later, reason will win out and cities will see they have no real choice but to adopt humane measures. And once they do, I suspect attitudes toward these birds will improve.

Truth be told, when I set out to write *Pigeons*, I was more interested in the humans who were obsessed with them, than the bird itself. Somewhere along the way that changed, and much like the book's audience, I became enthralled with these uncanny creatures.

Against my journalist's instincts, I have crossed the line from neutral observer to advocate, which is why I have teamed up with PETA to spread the gospel of humane pigeon control, as well as the Humane Society of the United States, to finally put an end to the barbaric live-pigeon shoots in Southeastern Pennsylvania. The three of us have also contacted New York City officials about the sleazy and inhumane practice of poaching pigeons for these Pennsylvanian gun clubs. Together, we've managed to raise awareness about these issues and help elevate the bird's status from "a worthless rat with wings," to something many urbanites and city officials around the country are willing to discuss without snickering.

But the humble pigeon's reputation still has a long way to go. Its status as war hero and goddess of fertility is seemingly forgotten, the bird is still persecuted daily. In Albany, New York, not far from where I live, a hospital hired a pest-control company, aptly named Rentokil, to poison dozens of roosting pigeons. The pigeons literally fell out of the sky and convulsed on the hospital grounds. It wasn't a pretty sight, nor was it particularly good publicity, but every few weeks I read about yet another city or town around the country adopting similarly cruel, yet ineffective, measures.

Meanwhile, a group of pigeon enthusiasts have been busy giving their sport a bad name. Federal agents arrested a dozen fanciers of Birmingham Rollers in several western states for trapping and killing thousands of falcons and hawks. Among those arrested was the president of the National Birmingham Rollers Club.

Birmingham Rollers have a genetic quirk that causes them to roll backward while in flight. It's a strangely beautiful thing to watch, especially when a whole flock of them tumbles backward nearly in unison, like a squadron of Blue Angels at an air show.

But these flight theatrics also attract the lethal attention of raptors. While it may be open season on pigeons, the Migratory Bird Treaty protects these birds of prey.

As usual, the Rock Dove continues to bring out the very best and the very worst in us. It's a creature that unwittingly engenders unusually strong passions, including the eccentric. One of my favorite e-mails I received from a reader was from a woman in California who sews her pet pigeons handsome cloth diapers. "Mr.Hooter's travels with me around town," she writes about one of her pigeons. "He has a leash and diaper that makes him as easy to be around as a dog. People are amazed, and can't believe he is a pigeon."

As I writer, I like to pride myself on describing my subjects in a visual manner, but after viewing one of my new pen pal's photos of a diapered pigeon, I can't deny that a picture can indeed be worth a thousand words.

My journey into pigeon fanaticism has rubbed off on me in more subtle ways. I'm unlikely to ever breed them, race them, or sew diapers for them, but I do like having them around. My family and I are spending the year in Dusseldorf, Germany, living in a fifth floor walk-up. We don't have a pet, nor is the wildlife particularly prevalent in this city. But to my toddler's delight (and my neighbor's dismay), we do have a handful of pigeons that visit us every morning to eat the small handful of bird seed we leave for them. There are other birds nearby, even wood pigeons, but none of them have the slightest interest in us.

The Rock Doves, however, are pleased to make our acquaintance.

—Andrew D. Blechman
July 2007
Dusseldorf, Germany
www.andrewblechman.com

Acknowledgments

I AM MOST GRATEFUL TO MY LITERARY AGENT CATHERINE Drayton, of Inkwell Management, without whom this book would have never come to be. While relaxing at a Vermont bed-and-breakfast, Catherine chanced upon an article that I had written about pigeon racing a year earlier for the *Smithsonian* magazine. She tracked me down to the Berkshires, where I was taking time off from writing to make ravioli, and persuaded me to write a book proposal. Thank you for your persistence, Catherine. Every writer should be so lucky.

When researching a book, one inevitably stumbles across some truly wonderful people. At the top of my list is the indefatigable Dr. Jean Hansell, a scholar, a charmer, and a most generous contributor to this book. It is through her superb books on dovecotes that I came to appreciate these nearly forgotten architectural gems. I highly recommend her books on pigeon history and iconography as well. Jean, I can think of no one with whom I'd rather climb a dusty, dung-encrusted dovecote.

My deepest thanks as well to my tremendously supportive parents, Laurel and Dietrich; my wonderful wife, Erika, who gave birth to, and patiently nurtured, Lillie

Annabelle, while this book was being written; my brilliant editor, Brando Skyhorse (the man with the coolest name in the business); Andrei Codrescu (for his gracious enthusiasm); the *Smithsonian* magazine; Daniel Maurer (for his keen eye); Richard Pine; and, of course, Morgan Entrekin.

The following people helped make this book possible: Dr. Gerald Lucas, Timothy W. Jaques, Erica L. Spizz, Tania Garcia, Stuart Braiman, Mark Greenfield, Donald H. Shaffer, Felice Picano, Marianne Maassen, Jeanette L. Maguire, Louis Moscatello, Holly Rockwell, Dr. Jack Ringler, Nick Griller, Bill Shein, Farm Girl Farm, Mark Hungate, Mark Jennings, Dana Cummings and Pete Baumann from the Simon's Rock College of Bard Alumni Library, and the ManKind Project. I would like to thank the Berkshire Co-op Market and the Berkshire South Regional Community Center for the sense of community these institutions cultivate; Brad Cooney and Michael Doss for tirelessly advocating for an interview with Mike Tyson; and Freddie Roach and Justin Fortune as well.

I would also like to thank the human subjects of this book; I can only hope that I've treated you fairly and with the dignity that, like the rock dove, you all deserve. I am particularly grateful to the following folks for answering my relentless questions: Jim Jenner of PACCOM Films, Muard Melvin MacRae Naugle, Jr., David Roth, Joseph De Scheemaecker, Frank and Ann Tasker, Carlo and Judy Napolitano, Prof. Richard F. Johnston of the University of Kansas, Prof. Charles Wolcott of Cornell University, Prof. Daniel Haag-Wackernagel of the University of Basel, Dr. Arturo Casadevall of the Albert Einstein College of Medicine, John Entwisle of Reuters, Emma Danby of Buckingham Palace, William, Melissa, and Katrina Byrne, the members of the New King's Lynn Pigeon Flying Club, the members of the Borough Park Homing Pigeon Club, Brian Newsome, David Staley, Joe Quinn, Stanley Mehr, Johanna Seeton, E. J. McAdams of New York City Audubon, Mindy Rosewitz of the U.S. Army Electronics Communications Museum at Fort Monmouth, Guy Merchant, the ever-dedicated Heidi Prescott of the Humane Society of the United States, Larry Reifsnyder, Andrew Kerns, Jack Wagner, David Kane, Al, Gila, and Bobbie Streit and their Pigeon People cohorts, the good people of FPRC and NYCPRC, Johanna Clearfield, Anna Dove, Sally Bananas, Eduardo Urbina, Bob from B.O.B., Gordon King, and Tony Barwick and Christie Hadwin of the Palmetto Pigeon Plant. I'd also like to thank Kee Bubbenmoyer. While I cannot condone your hobby, I do appreciate your trust and hospitality. If I've forgotten someone, please accept my apologies.

Finally, I'd like to thank Orlando and Omayra Martinez for opening up your lives to me, and José Martinez for sharing a bite with me at the corner bodega on a miserable slushy afternoon. It was perhaps the most fortuitous tuna sandwich I have ever eaten.